Henry May

Speech of Hon. Henry May of Maryland

Delivered in the House of representatives

Henry May

Speech of Hon. Henry May of Maryland
Delivered in the House of representatives

ISBN/EAN: 9783337235307

Printed in Europe, USA, Canada, Australia, Japan

Cover: Foto ©Suzi / pixelio.de

More available books at **www.hansebooks.com**

SPEECHES

OF THE

HON. HENRY MAY,

OF MARYLAND,

DELIVERED IN THE

HOUSE OF REPRESENTATIVES,

At the Third Session of the Thirty-Seventh Congress.

BALTIMORE:

PRINTED BY KELLY, HEDIAN & PIET,

No. 174 BALTIMORE STREET.

1863.

EULOGY.

The death of the Hon. JAMES ALFRED PEARCE, late Senator from Maryland, having been announced in the House of Representatives, on the 13th of January, 1863,

Mr. MAY, of Maryland, said :

MR. SPEAKER : I have only been apprised since I came into this Hall, that these sad ceremonies of respect to our distinguished colleague, were appointed for to-day. I wish, sir, to offer my tribute to his memory. He honored me with his friendship for many years, and in the last months of his life freely imparted to me his views upon the vital questions which now, unhappily, divide our country. I am authorized to speak for him here upon those questions; and I wish, if the unpremeditated thoughts and feelings suggested by the occasion, or awakened by the touching and eloquent tributes of the distinguished gentlemen who have preceded me, may go in place of more studied eulogy, to offer them just as they spring from my heart. I desire to speak of the respect in which he was held by those who, in the divisions of political sentiment, as represented in party organization, having opposed him throughout the greater portion of his life, at length discovering that he was a public man who followed " principles, and not men," honored him with the highest testimony of their confidence, and committed to him the representation of the sovereignty of their State. For the Democratic party of the State of Maryland, I speak ; and also for those of all parties who believed with him that the Constitution of this land was made for war as well as for peace ; nay, sir, who believe that its strongest and most priceless sanctions were designed as bulwarks against the tendencies of arbitrary power supported by military authority, and therefore have a higher obligation in war than in peace. For those in our State who, while acknowledging all the delegated powers of the Federal Government, yet retain an equal reverence and respect for the reserved rights of the States, I also bear testimony of their respect for his distinguished public life—a life which illustrated, in a long public service, all those virtues which can adorn a high and pure-minded republican Representative. For all these classes of our fellow-citizens, I wish to pay the tribute of their respect for his character and public services, and to express their profound sorrow for his death.

Mr. Speaker, when the storms of passion had prostrated the assembled Representatives in both Halls of this Capitol, our Senator stood, amid the few, firm and erect. Broken in health, his vital powers almost exhausted, he yet marched up with the remnant of his life to the side of the bleeding Constitution of his country, and gave his latest efforts to sustain it. He did all that a public man could do here to support the paramount authority of the Constitution, and to oppose and defy the exertions of arbitrary power. I remember with infinite pleasure, and repeat it here with delight, that one of the last efforts of his public service was a noble speech vindicating his fellow-citizens of Maryland against the criminal and cruel oppressions under which they were then suffering. I remember how his heart, the seat of his fatal disease, pulsating with a noble enthusiasm and sympathy for them, and beating too warmly, denied him the utterance of speech, and compelled him to retire from the Senate and seek the quiet of his chamber; and well do I remember another most gratifying instance of his spirit of liberty. It was my duty, as a Representative of the State of Maryland, to take counsel of his experience in one of the rooms of the Capitol, touching an atrocious and unparalleled outrage on the judiciary of our State, by dragging from the bench an honored, eminent, and faithful magistrate, scattering his blood upon the ermine, and well nigh taking his life by the hands of armed ruffians; and I can never forget the glow of indignation that kindled his eye and swelled his breast at the recital of the facts. The excitement was too strong for his enfeebled frame, and he sunk under the exhaustion of his own noble enthusiasm. If he could do no more to vindicate the authority of the Constitution of his country than he did accomplish, it was because he was denied the power to do it by the prostration of his vital functions, and the unheeding passions that prevailed. The worthless tenement of flesh could not support the struggles of its undying guest. Sir, he felt that it was his duty to prevent and redress, and not invite or provoke, the further aggressions of a reckless tyranny. He so stated his views to me.

Mr. Speaker, let no advocate of unlicensed power, dare claim an approbation of his views because this eminent Senator did not wrestle more conspicuously with arbitrary power in the halls of Congress; nor let any complaining victim of tyranny question the integrity or the noble devotion of his services in their behalf; nor yet must any self-applauding martyr of liberty, attempt to gain a passing notoriety at the expense of the fame of this departed statesman of Maryland; but let these, and all of us, draw from the contemplation of his life, on this solemn occasion, instruction that may be salutary. Let us learn from the moderation and fidelity of his character, to admire in our public stations, and seek those duties which look to conciliation, compromise, and concord. Let no wrongs suffered, no resentment fixed in our breasts, move us from the discharge of these sacred duties; but let us try, through the common suffering that afflicts the land, to walk out from the dominion of passion, purified, regenerated and disenthralled.

I trust, Mr. Speaker, that, speaking from my heart, as I ought to speak on an occasion like this, I trespass not against the limits which ought to be observed in discussing the virtues of an eminent statesman. I must speak now, sir, as I feel. While commending to public praise and respect the memory and services of this distinguished man, I must be allowed to distinguish him as one who, having sworn to support the Constitution of his country, to the latest moment of his life, and through every trial, kept the faith of that obligation to his Maker and his fellow citizens. He rests, now, near the banks of the Chesapeake. The flowers which the distinguished gentleman from Kentucky described so beautifully as surrounding his grave, are symbols not only of his taste, but also of his immortality. And may we not trust, too, that the blossoms and fruits which opened and adorned his life here, will also be more gloriously unfolded and ripened in a higher and brighter sphere.

Mr. Speaker, while we deplore the loss of such public characters in this time of our national afflictions, may we not inquire why, in the inscrutable decrees of Providence, those gifted, experienced, and good men, whose lives were consecrated to the public service and to the welfare of their fellow-men, are removed from us? We cannot presume to penetrate the mysteries of divine wisdom. We must accept those providential lessons as teaching us that the cup of our adversity is not yet full; that the chastening rod is not yet to be broken; and also solemnly admonishing us that passion is perhaps yet longer to have its sway. But are we not authorized to call upon those ascended statesmen who, like him, have passed from earth; all those great and good men who devoted their lives and talents to establish and maintain the principles embodied in our Constitution, which not only form the bond of our union, but which are higher and infinitely more priceless than it; those principles of civil liberty which form the foundations on which the whole fabric of the happiness of man under every form of free government rests? May we not expect, I repeat, that the spirits of the great statesmen who formed this noble structure of our government, and those who came after them and supported its pure and faithful administration— ay, sir, and the thousands of citizens whose souls have gone from ensanguined battle-fields—will be assembled witnesses at the bar of Heaven, pleading the cause of their bleeding country, and that the Almighty Ruler of all nations, responding in His good time, will send down His angel of peace among us? Such, sir, is my devout prayer.

SPEECH

OF THE

HON. HENRY MAY, OF MARYLAND,

AGAINST

THE WAR AND ARMING NEGROES,

AND FOR

PEACE AND RECOGNITION.

In the House of Representatives, February 2d, 1863.

The House having under consideration bill No. 675, to raise additional soldiers for the service of the Government—

Mr. MAY said:

Mr. SPEAKER,—The respect that I feel for the people of the State I in part represent; my knowledge of their feelings, their interests, and, I believe, their ultimate determination, require me to state some objections to this measure. With respect to the relations of this question as one of Federal power, I am dismissed from all obligation to consider it. As propounding a scheme of military strength, the bill is simply preposterous. As an evidence of national policy, it is eminently disgraceful. Sir, it will fail, and the enlightened opinion of mankind will pronounce upon the attempt a condign judgment. To us who are familiar with the characteristics of the African race, these theories that sentimental gentlemen on the other side so frequently present, but serve to amuse. Their ideas of the perfectibility of the negro are another lesson to instruct us in that mortal presumption which raises questions with eternal power, and challenges the plans of the Creator.

Sir, I never hear these platitudes sounded in this Hall and intended to elevate the negro to the same scale of being with the white man, without recognizing an attempt to overthrow those gradations which He has established in the distributions of intellect, and am reminded of the admonitions of that noble Essay on Man, which I beg leave now to repeat for the edification of these gentlemen :

> " Go, wiser thou, and in thy scale of sense
> Weigh thy opinion against Providence,
> Call imperfection what thou fanciest such ;
> Say, here He gives too little, there too much.
> Destroy all creatures for thy sport or gust,
> And cry, if man's unhappy, God's unjust ;
> If man alone engross not Heaven's high care,
> Alone made mortal here, immortal there,
> Snatch from His hand the balance and the rod,
> Rejudge His justice, be the God of God."

Sir, we who recognize the amiable disposition of the domesticated African, his inert nature, his slovenly habits, his clumsiness, his want of vigilance, and his timidity, know that of all human beings he presents the least qualifications for a soldier. Go to your soldiers at Port Royal, New Orleans, or Hampton, and ask them what they think of this, and they will tell you that the effort to erect the domesticated African into a soldier is a preposterous exhibition of human presumption and folly. Mr. Speaker, we are informed that his sable majesty, the King of Dahomey, has raised up around him, in the savage instincts of his race, an army tremendously invincible, but cruel beyond all parallel in the records of history, savage or civilized. Is it the King of Dahomey whose example is to be presented here for our adoption in this enlightened, civilized, and Christian land? Do gentlemen consider, when they refer to instances of the employment of the negro in the war of the Revolution, or by that great commander at New Orleans, that there he was engaged in fighting on the side of his virtues? And do they not see that the proposition here is an attempt to array him on the side of his vices, and make him emulate the ferocious diplays of the King of Dahomey, or the horrors of San Domingo?

The people of Maryland recoil with abhorrence from a proposition that may lead to such results. They are startled by it. The civilized, enlightened, and Christianized world will condemn to unmitigated scorn that legislation which would plant on our statute-books a measure so infamous and infernal. Do we not recollect the thrill of instinctive emotion with which we have listened, when children, to the rehearsal of that noble philippic which Lord Chatham delivered against the proposition to employ savages in the war against our forefathers? The impulses which responded to the noble eloquence of that great orator were but the strong and emphatic admonitions of nature, against measures so revolting to humanity. I do not hesitate to say that rather than these furies shall be let loose upon our countrymen " like Até fresh from hell," the people of my State will plant themselves in a defiant opposition to those who, regardless of every obligation, both human and divine, have summoned such demoniacal agencies to maintain their power.

But, independently of the grounds of objection I have stated, I am also opposed to this measure because I am opposed to the war. I wish briefly to present my views on this ground of objection. I wish to do so with a feeling of profound grief for the situation of our country. No views of a personal nature; no feelings of resentment or of disappointment shall mingle with my thoughts; no captious criticisms, nor yet a factious design, shall mar the sincere views that I now propose to present. I approach with diffidence and apprehension, the appalling condition of our bleeding country, and see—

" How nations sink, by darling schemes oppressed,
When vengeance listens to the fool's request."

I would avoid the contemplation of its sufferings, and, if I could resist the claims of duty, forbear to try the difficult and embarrassing path before me.

I came here a Representative of peace and compromise, and the determined adversary of military coercion. No party claimed my nomination; but a short statement of my views was accepted; and the people I have the honor to represent bestowed their confidence and elected me. No party hailed my election, and I entered this Hall an independent Representative of peace, conciliation and compromise. Foreseeing the futility of arms in such a contest as was then impending, and believing that the ruin which now seems so inevitable would follow the cruel strife that was to cleave open the hearts of kindred and of countrymen by each other's hands, in countless numbers, I have opposed and voted against every measure of this war. Not a drop of the blood of my countrymen rests upon me. An advocate of peace from the first, and always, let no man, now that the sorrows of our nation rise up to Heaven appealing for its sanctions, challenge or condemn my devotion to its real interests.

At the first called session of this Congress, and after the terrible lesson of Manassas had, as I fondly hoped, opened through the vistas of a bloody and hopeless future of strife, contemplations of peace, I felt it was my duty to propose, at once, a plan of adjustment. I did so; but it met with no favor here.° Passion was yet longer to rule the sad destinies of our once happy land; and anger, hate, revenge, cold, calculating avarice, too, and foul corruption, tainting the very air, these were yet to hold an undisputed sway.

Sir, it will be recollected that I then predicted the employment " of the cruel and merciless means" that are now presented for our adoption. And my Democratic friends will do me the justice to recollect the earnest effort I made to warn

---

*At the extra session of this Congress, Mr. MAY offered the following, (see Congressional Globe, first session, Thirty-seventh Congress, page 445:)

" Whereas the Government of the United States of America was created by its written Constitution, and derived its just powers alone from the consent of the people, as contained in that instrument, and it has no other powers, and force and arms can neither preserve nor rightfully be permitted to violate its Constitution under any authority whatsoever; and whereas Washington and other great sages and patriots, who founded our General Government, solemnly warning their countrymen, predicted its destruction from the establishment of a sectional political party; and they also entreated a spirit of compromise whenever necessary to preserve the Union; and whereas a civil war now exists among the States which have been united, which, having already prostrated the peace, prosperity, and happiness of the people, and destroyed many valuable citizens, now threatens their destruction in countless numbers, and by its inevitable tendency, if not necessity, the final overthrow of free constitutional government: Therefore,

" 1. Be it Resolved, That the success of the Republican party, founded, as it is, on a sectional, social, and political question, is justly responsible for the origin of our present national misfortunes.

" 2. That the uncompromising spirit hitherto manifested by the representatives of that party has prevented a peaceful compromise and adjustment of our unhappy difficulties when the same was practicable.

" 3. That if the present war continues, the only safety and refuge of constitutional government and civil liberty will be found in the constitutions and sovereignty of the several States, and afterwards, through them, the only hope of a future and more harmonious reconstruction of the Union.

" 4. That it is impossible for arms to subjugate the people of the seceded States, united as they are in such numbers, so fully prepared and resolved, and actuated by motives which represent the just pride and dignity of equals, of trained freemen, of American citizens; and also believing, as they do to a man, that State, home, wife, children, property, all and every security and benefit of Government is at stake, and that the most cruel and merciless means, forced by the necessities of an exhausting and desolating war, are to be employed against them.

" 5. That in view of all these public calamities, and to avoid them, recognizing the necessities which control human affairs, as our fathers of the Revolution did, it becomes the duty of Congress, before it closes its present session, to provide for the appointment of commissioners to procure an armistice between the contending armies, and restore peace at all events; and who shall be empowered to arrange a compromise to preserve the Union, if possible; but if not, then a peaceful separation of the respective States of the Union, as well such as now claim to have seceded, as others which may by the sovereign will of their citizens also hereafter ordain to secede; and that the said commissioners be solemnly enjoined so to conduct their negotiations as to obtain, if possible, in the future, a happy, harmonious, and perpetual re-construction of our Union of States.

" Mr. BINGHAM. I propose to debate that resolution.

" The SPEAKER. Then it must go over.

" Mr. MAY. I move to suspend the rules, for the purpose of allowing the resolution to be considered at this time.

" Mr. LOVEJOY. I raise a question upon the reception of the resolution, that it is not within the order adopted by the House at the commencement of the session.

" The SPEAKER. The gentleman from Maryland moves to suspend the rules, which is in order, it being within the last ten days of the session.

" Mr. MAY demanded the yeas and nays upon his motion to suspend the rules.

" The yeas and nays were not ordered; only seven members having voted therefor."

them against becoming pledged to the support of a war " which would require them to disguise their civilization with the paint of the savage, and pursuing the war paths of this Administration, seize the tomahawk and scalping knife," results from which they now so instinctively recoil.

The present condition of our country can find no parallel in history. In vain can an example be searched for. A people the freest and happiest of the earth, we were blessed with the best Government that ever has existed. Providence seemed to have preserved our continent undiscovered until the progress of the principles of free government were sufficiently matured by the wise and good of the earth, to make America the appointed place for their development and happy trial. The circumstances of our settlement, the various types of the early emigrants, the differences of religion, of habits, manners, customs, and institutions, all these conspired to help the hopeful problem. And when the purifying fires of our glorious Revolution lit up the high motives and exalted the natures that made the patriot and the hero of 1789, then all that Heaven could do, and more than it had ever before vouchsafed to man, was done, to erect the noblest structure of a free government that had blessed the earth. Those patriot heroes did the rest. Consummate wisdom and a noble disinterestedness of purpose, guided by moderation, conciliation, and a spirit of compromise, enabled these great men to finish the grand work of our majestic Constitution. Those who came next after them imitated their virtues and followed their example. The Government of the United States flourished, expanded, and became at length the admitted equal of the greatest of earthly Powers, the most admired of nations,

" The land of the free and the home of the brave."

Unexampled prosperity and power had been gained. The oppressed of the world hailed our asylum of liberty, and the divine right of monarchs began " to pale its ineffectual fires " before the radiant splendor of our new Republic. The present and the future, the citizen and the sojourner, the emigrant, the sighing children of liberty everywhere hailed our United States as the perfection of human government.

But, sir, the necessities of labor and the cupidity of commerce sowed the fatal seeds of our discord. The ill-fated children of Africa, though led out from the captivity of barbarism, darkened as by a shadow the bright focus of our cultivation and finally have eclipsed it; and strangely and mysteriously the barbarism of Africa seems now about to subdue the civilization of America.

African slavery was established in all the colonies, and those who are now engaged in destroying it, have inherited and enjoyed the wealth it helped to create. Climate and soil unsuited to the negro slave banished him from New England and the North to the warmer regions of the South, and " a compensated emancipation " from a fruitless dominion, fully satisfied all the demands of conscience or humanity. There was then no sin in bringing these human chattels from their native shores—in originating their sad enslavement, or in parting from it for money. " The precious price told down" then purged the moral sight, and slavery stood only revealed in hideous wickedness when interest stepped aside and was released. Sir, foreseeing this result and fearing it, the founders of our system provided every security against it. Before the Union could be established, the strongest and most binding covenants that man can make in forms of government were provided, and faith, sacred faith in these guards of slavery, were mutually given and accepted. No stronger obligation can man give to man than our Constitution provides for this. It is in vain, sir, to consider any other or further guarantees. If these be not strong enough, if faith such as this is to be broken, then there is nothing of human institution that can endure, and we find the inevitable end of free consented Government.

The sin of slavery, if it be such, may be carried by a "higher law" to Heaven; but here upon this earth of ours, faith, the bond, the law, the Constitution—these are its justifications. Our present national afflictions are the direct results of an intermeddling spirit at the North. Over and over again have the slaveholding States argued, remonstrated, appealed in every way, by every effort, to restrain the aggressive spirit of the North from these invasions on its rights of domestic slavery; and though often passion has defied and denounced its progress, reason has not failed to use its persuasive power. Compromise after compromise has been made, in the hope of averting or postponing the evil day of apprehended separation. Sir, the convulsions of these attempts were the disregarded warnings of our present calamity. For years, for many years, have patient, thoughtful statesmen and patriots from North and South, in most impressive lessons, warned our countrymen, and predicted our present situation as the inevitable result of these aggressions. But, alas, in vain. Instigated by the earnestness and success of a small but mischievous party of fanatics, the lust of political power at the North, at length seized upon the subject of slavery, and employed its humanitarian aspects for the mere sake of office, or the rewards of party success; regardless of all the most sacred obligations of Government—thus establishing a general and defiant spirit of lawlessness which, habitually aggressing upon the plainest rights of equality, left no hope of future peace and security to the South. And while slavery was to be abolished at all events, yet no one among its wisest enemies at the North was able to discover a practicable plan for the future disposal of the emancipated slave; nor, sir, to this hour has any such plan been provided. And while the non-slaveholding States are equally responsible for the existence of slavery among us, and are confessedly unable to relieve its evils—if such there are—and the slaveholding States are equally powerless to remove them, we yet find that such plans of alleviation and ultimate relief as the policy of their laws or schemes of colonization have attempted, have been thwarted by the mischievous designs of the people of the North. The more improved and cultivated black man being refused a residence among them by the policy of the laws of some of the free States, resulting from the evils attending such residence, yet nevertheless these disinterested citizens of such States would inflict the greater evils of a permanent abode of the half-civilized negro among the people of the South. Delivering themselves by a gradual process from the evils attending the abolition of slavery, they propose, suddenly and without preparation, to set free the slaves of the South, and bring inevitable ruin upon the interests dependent upon their labor; nay, more than this, would instigate the forceful brutal passions of the slave, on principles "of self-defense," as the proclamation insidiously presents it, to take the torch, or poison, or the knife against sleeping wife and children.

Mr. Speaker, it was the settled conviction in the minds of the people of the South that such were the plans of the people of the North, and that the Federal power was to be the instrument of such savage aggressions, that caused the secession of their States. They felt, and all who understand the subject know how just and natural was the feeling, that such a state of constant and increasing apprehension had rendered the influence of the General Government insupportable. They felt that not only Government, but even life itself was not worth having, upon the terms of such habitual strife, anxiety, and alarm—the Government of the United States had failed, or was about to fail, in those great objects of "establishing justice," "insuring domestic tranquility," and "promoting the general welfare," and which concerned so vitally their rights and happiness ; and they resolved to separate from a Government they could no longer either trust or endure. Sir, they did complain of the injustice that sectional interests of manufactures or of commerce had inflicted ; but the influence of this complaint, while it added to the prevailing discontent by ascribing a selfish and domineering spirit to the North, offensive to ideas of equality, and raising up views of incompatible and conflicting interests ; yet these causes alone could never have separated our Union.

If the existence of these destructive influences has been heretofore denied, is there not now too much reason to feel convinced that, however concealed, they have existed? Do not the feelings and motives that are signified in these measures now presented, and in the kindred transactions of Congress and the Executive, give every true lover of republican government the right to say, that what was a rebellion against law now stands justified before God, and the nations of the earth, as a revolution against the most direful oppressions that have ever threatened mankind? Happily, however, sir, those whom the calamities of war have most afflicted, are to be spared the terrible vengeance now denounced against them ; and the menaces of the proclamation and of these measures are turned into an invincible sword of defense. But loyal Maryland, Kentucky, Missouri, and Delaware, these so proclaimed and praised for their devotion, are to be the victims ; faithful and defenseless, the sword of the presidential wrath pierces their vitals through the sides of the bleeding Constitution which they have so faithfully supported.

I repeat, it was the settled conviction of the southern slaveholding States that an "irrepressible conflict" did actually exist between them and the people and States of the North, and which was promoted by the latter ; that "all must be free or all slave ;" "that a house divided against itself cannot stand." Sir, it was the conviction forced upon the people of the South, that these emphatic enunciations of opinion were but the "slogans" of an inevitable oppression that was fast approaching, was then in effect inaugurated with authority and power, which could not be averted, and would, unless at once resisted, attack and destroy their sacred rights of personal liberty, of personal security, and private property, the fundamental rights of man, and for which, if he will not give battle, he deserves to lose.

They believed that the North was abolitionized, and had consequently abjured the obligations of any covenant with slavery, however solemnly made. This it was that made them renounce their allegiance and withdraw from the Union.

Before the Supreme Judge of the world they opened their hearts and resolved to offer up to Him the responsibilities of their cause upon the field of battle. Sir, have not enough bleeding souls testified to these convictions in Heaven already? Have we not, their countrymen, their fellow-men, received enough assurance of their sincerity, their devotion, their power? Must this desolating war yet go on?

This solemn and momentous inquiry now tortures the thoughts and anxieties of the just and the good. I am persuaded that the voice of all civilized and disinterested men is now on the side of peace—peace on any terms consistent with our liberties and honor.

Let me, sir, briefly explore, with hopeful view, this pleasing inquiry—

"The cause of truth, and human weal,
O God above,
Transfer it from the sword's appeal
To peace and love."

Before I venture upon this, I wish to declare in all candor, as I ought to do, my settled conviction, that the people of the confederated States will never again consent to restore our political Union. I believe that their universal determination upon this point, is final. They will not again put their trust in the guarantees of a written Constitution with the people of the North. They have tried it fairly, and it has failed. Sir, they believe, and I believe, that there is established a fixed and unalterable antagonism between the sections where slavery is and is not allowed, and that no future political Union, so long as slavery exists, can ever be maintained between them upon any basis whatever.

It is folly now to expect it. The part of wisdom and of duty requires us to accept this irreversible conclusion; and however it may disappoint our hopes or interests, or mortify our pride, we ought *at once*, in the precept of our own great Declaration of Independence, " to acquiesce in the necessity that denounces our separation;" to cast the plans of our future, by the light it yet affords, or midnight darkness and utter ruin may ere long claim our republican destinies.

Mr. Speaker, that eminent and far-seeing statesman, the late Judge Douglas, avowed to me in April preceding his death, his solemn conviction that our political Union was at an end. I violate no confidence in repeating his opinions, since he assured me it was his purpose to publish his views at an early day; and if the sequel of his life may seem in conflict with these views, there are those among his personal friends, here on this floor, who can reconcile his conduct, and show the conformity of his plans with a peaceful, though it might be a revolutionary solution, of our national troubles. Judge Douglas, on that occasion, read to me an elaborate essay, which he told me had cost him more thought and labor than any work of his life; that he feared it was too long, and he wished both to abridge and simplify it, so that it might be read and understood by all; that he would revise it at Chicago and then give it to his countrymen. Death, alas! frustrated this most patriotic design. That essay ascribed our present situation to the aggressive spirit of northern abolitionism. It declared his conviction that the Union of our States as originally formed and maintained, was finally destroyed, and no political Union could exist again between the free and slaveholding States: that such an idea must be adandoned, and a *commercial Union*, founded upon the plan generally, of the zollverein of the States of Germany, be accepted, as the only practicable arrangement to secure peace now and hereafter. That masterly paper, every word of which I heard read by himself, and which since his death, I have endeavored in vain to procure, for the benefit of its wise counsels to our countrymen, fully explained the plan, operation, and results of the zollverein, and showed how, with certain modifications, it could be adapted to sustain all those principal causes and influences which have hitherto made the United States the happiest and most prosperous of nations.

And now, sir, let me inquire what has been gained by the prosecution of the war? With an enormous disparity of forces and resources in favor of the Federal Government, are we nearer the end of the conflict than when we began. Does the present prospect of military affairs give encouragement of a speedy or even successful termination of the strife? It must be confessed by all candid minds that these inquiries cannot be answered in a way favorable to the cause of the Union. Besides the results of a few ineffectual victories, the invasion of the enemy's country, and the capture of New Orleans or less important towns, what has been done but to destroy or maim thousands of men, and waste or consume millions of property, and entail upon ourselves and posterity the burdens of an insupportable taxation? The present generation of young, gallant, and hopeful men, with all their divine right to a long and happy life, cut down like grass before the scythe, and scattered in unknown graves, and the next generation, already bowed with affliction, and struggling from the loss of those whose protecting hands this desolating war has folded beneath the sod, they, too, must add to their griefs, the toilsome burdens of a life-long taxation, and dying, transmit it to their children's children.

I have said, sir, that the judgment of the impartial nations of Europe has already pronounced this war a failure. Are we too vain, or too proud to be instructed by these testimonies before our eyes? Must multiplying visions of the dead, the dying, the maimed, or wounded, or sick, yet pass in endless procession before our sorrowing eyes? Are our ears yet longer to be filled with the agonies of the poor chilled fireside and home? Are our tears still to flow for these broken hearts, these bereaved women and little children? And, sir, are we here again to measure the toils and miseries of bowed down labor in renewing exhausting tax bills or repeating schemes of revenue? I trust not; but hope, by the favor of Heaven, we may at once be spared these horrors, and rejoice to see once more the halcyon gleams of peace.

Mr. Speaker, if this war is to go on, it can only end on the one hand, in the subjugation of the South, followed by perpetual strife, the extermination of the white or black race, the evils of an immense standing army, and the utter extinction of civil liberty there, if not here; or on the other, in recognition of the confederate States as a nation, followed, if we are wise, by re-established intercourse and commercial relations, reconciling conflicting interests, and which, while preserving peace at home, will, at the same time, secure a union against foreign aggression, and be the only means, by the softening influences they will present, of restoring any political relations in the future. Sir, a commercial union is all that is left for us to consider; a political union is utterly impossible. The sovereignty of the States, their constitutions and laws, the complete systems of government ordained and maintained by them will secure every political right, or if not, the delegated powers of the Federal or Confederated systems may accomplish this. The material interests, the benefits of commerce, will be developed and secured by an American zollverein, while the moral or social antagonisms which have produced the war, or are produced by it, will find their only protection in the authorities of international law; and all the sin of slavery, all accountability for it here and hereafter, will be forever washed away from the shrinking and sensitive souls of the North.

Separation, RECOGNITION, dissolving finally all political and moral relations with the non-slaveholding States, now offers the healing balm to the wounded breast of the political abolitionist. The earnest struggle his devotion has made attests its intensity in the council and the field, and the God of battles who hath watched his glowing zeal will vindicate the heroism of his efforts. Let his conscience then be calmed.

Sir, the domestic law—the Constitution and its paper sanctions—has proved too weak for human passion—or conscience, if you please—and the law of nations and its dread arbiter, the sword, must hereafter keep the peace of our North American continent.

Mr. Speaker, what can this civil war accomplish? If the experience of the past may answer, it will exclaim, ruin, nothing but ruin, fighting, bloodshed, lamentation, desolation, anarchy, despotism. Must it still go on—

" Never ending, still beginning,
Fighting still, and still destroying.

If, sir, the sword is yet to continue the dread arbiter between us, while I do not undervalue the courage of the Federal troops, I must yet ask you to consider the motives, the strength, and resources of the Confederates.

The fatal policy that a blind fanaticism has directed here and from the White House, has supplied all that was wanting at the South. I do know when I say that the despondency which denounced the advent of the Mayflower, and characterized it as, next to the fall of Adam, the greatest evil that had afflicted man, was relieved when the proclamation of ruin was made against every right of property, of liberty, of security at the South. I do know, that when conscription acts were arraying the opposition not only of the people, but of States, and bringing despair to the hopes of the South, these proclamations raised up armed men as volunteers from every spot of ground, and added ten to defend the fireside, where conscription demanded five for the confederation. Have you considered, sir, with the motives now engaged at the South in supporting this fearful contest, the influence this policy must naturally exert over the minds of the Federal troops? Does the executioner avert his face when the axe falls upon the sincere and concientious, though it may be, erring life of a countryman? Sir, the Judge, the President, the Cabinet, the Congress who pronounce the doom may sit cold and impassive, removed from the scene; but neither the soldier of the cross or of republican liberty, of Christianity or civilization, will aid to strike down home and wife and children. Not an American soldier, not one man, with a soul fit for the destinies of heaven, will execute the horrors demanded by these proclamations. Manhood recoiling from such infernal service, the soldiers themselves will stop this war before raising their hands to help the merciless and inevitable fate denounced against sleeping women and helpless children. Is there a heart of man South, ay, sir, or North, that will not pour out its last drop in such a cause ?

In that memorable speech on conciliation with America, delivered in the British Parliament by the great Burke, he discovered some views of our nature that may now prove instructive. Speaking for peace then, as I do now, and enumerating the influences that distinguished the people of our northern and southern colonies, he said :

" Sir, I can perceive by their manner that some gentlemen object to the latitude of this description ; because in the southern colonies the Church of England forms a large body, and has a regular establishment. It is certainly true. There is, however, a circumstance attending these colonies which, in my opinion, fully counterbalances this difference, and makes the spirit of liberty still more high and haughty than in those to the northward. It is that in Virginia and the Carolinas they have a vast multitude of slaves. Where this is the case in any part of the world, those who are free, are by far the most proud and jealous of their freedom. Freedom is to them not only an enjoyment, but a kind of rank and privilege. Not seeing there that freedom as in countries where it is a common blessing, and as broad and general as the air, may be united with much abject toil, with great misery, with all the exterior of servitude, liberty looks, among them, like something that is more noble and liberal. I do not mean, sir, to commend the superior morality of this sentiment, which has at least as much pride as virtue in it ; but I cannot alter the nature of the man. The fact is so; and these people of the southern colonies are much more strongly, and with a higher and more stubborn spirit, attached to liberty, than those to the northward. Such were all the ancient commonwealths; such were our Gothic ancestors ; such in our days were the Poles ; and such will be all masters of slaves who are not slaves themselves. In such a people the haughtiness of domination combines with the spirit of freedom, fortifies it, and renders it invincible."

Sir, the people of the North are profoundly ignorant equally of the nature and characteristics of the white citizen of the South as they are of the nature and characteristics of the negro.

Why, sir, if it be ascertained that we can no longer be united in harmony, in peace, bringing prosperity and happiness in their train, why should a union be enforced ?

If the consent of the governed, the consent of so considerable a portion as those are who have now dissolved their political relations, be refused ; why compel at such fearful cost a union with burning hate, revenge, and eternal discord ? There is no free republican Union, no real union of our American States or people but such as free consent gives, bringing a willing obedience, loyalty, and the principles of public virtue to support it. No other is either worth creating or worth preserving. These, sir, were the sentiments of our forefathers, and will be of our posterity. If they are not ours, it is because we are blinded by passion.

Mr. Speaker, we are told that the Almighty fixes the boundaries of nations ; that the rock-ribbed mountains and the flowing rivers are the eternal ligaments that, binding men together in one union, mark the limits of political States, and which, being the work of His hands, we must not presumptuously venture to disturb ; that geography and the physical things of the earth, and not its peoples, are the subjects of government.

This, sir, is a beautiful theory, and admirable for its moral design ; but, the history of man and his governments from the beginning of the world refutes it.

" What constitutes a State?
Not high raised battlements, or labor'd mound,
    Thick wall, or moated gate;
Not cities proud, with spires and turrets crown'd;
    Not bays and broad arm'd ports,
Where, laughing at the storm, rich navies ride :
    Nor starr'd and spangled courts,
Where low-brow'd baseness wafts perfumes to pride—
    No! men, high-minded men,
 .   .   *   *   .   *   .   *
    Men who their duties know,
But know their rights; and knowing, dare maintain,
    Prevent the long-aimed blow,
And crush the tyrant, while they rend the chain—
    These constitute a State."

Mr. Speaker, I do not propose to enter further into this inquiry than to point to the records geography herself unfolds, all round the world, to overthrow this asserted power. I do not venture to deny the influence that the laws of nature exert in fixing the boundaries of nations; but, sir, I dispute their presiding power. The limits that separated our colonies, the pride and dominion of State power, and even the now warring spirit of secession, are but so many proofs that the reformed institutions we have attempted to establish in this New World of ours, can find no preserving aid in the physical plans of our Creator.

However pleasing to our hopes, or soothing to our anxieties, we must dismiss these delusive ideas. Our honorable love of empire, or of union, must yield to the nature of man, and, until we can alter it, be contented to find the jurisdictions, at least of free government, in those boundaries his consent, or his passions have fixed.

Can all the rain that falls upon the Alleghany's sides; can the swift torrents, or the tides that swell the banks of the Potomac, or Rappahannock, or Cumberland, or Mississippi, wash away from kindred hearts the memories of the precious blood this cruel war has shed? Can mountains hide from sorrowing eyes those graveyard highways that stretch across the land—

" Where every turf beneath the feet
Hath been a soldier's sepulchre?"

or rivers sink beneath their beds the whitened bones, that choke their channels up? Can home, and all its fond endearments, smouldering in ashes, be forgotten? Can the agony of the broken heart be cured? Can flaming anger, hate, revenge, be soothed; or pride, ambition, glory, all subdued? No, Mr. Speaker; you may subjugate, exterminate the southern people, but until you can tear out each living heart and throw it to the dogs of war, you can never reunite them with you in a political union.

I shall not stoop to consider in a comparison with the profound motives I have here presented, the questions of material interest that may be involved, or count in mercenary measures the precious lives of my countrymen.

Sir, the vital principle of our Union is consent and not force; and when I hear the advocates of the latter appealing to " the nation " and " its unity," I recognize at once the insidious arguments for a centralized power to be erected upon the ruins of the Republic. And, the views that find inevitable force in the arrangements of our physical geography, have, I fear, the same unhappy tendency.

Until my honorable friend from Ohio (Mr. Vallandigham)—whose powerful arguments for peace I so much admire, and whose sincere devotion to his country I have so much reason to know—can "alter the nature of man," he will pardon me for rejecting, as I do, the bright hopes he presents.

It is the part of wisdom and of duty to recognize the necessities that control all human affairs. If we cannot restore all that is lost, let us at least preserve what is left. If we cannot re-establish a political union, let us, while saving our constitutional liberties, retrieve a union for peace and for commerce.

Mr. Speaker, the question now before us is between separation and subjugation. Let us not deceive ourselves. We must choose between these fearful alternatives, and take the olive branch, or closer clutch the sword. I have made, sir, my choice, and intend to abide its issue. As I have from the first, so I will to the last, stand by the side of peace and constitutional liberty. Rather than the havoc of this desolating war with its appalling effects shall be longer continued, I would prefer to see the Union, the States, counties, cities, and towns, with their governments all separated and dissolved, if peacefully, into the elements of society or of nature ; and trust to find in the wants of my fellowmen, undebauched by the lawlessness of war, yet purified by the adversity of their failure, the principles and motives of a more harmonious reconstruction of government. Rather than meet the anarchy or despotism, or both, that are now so surely approaching us in the background of this fraternal strife to destroy the few remaining sanctions of our Constitution, and sink every hope of any union and all free government, I for one would at once stop this war, and, RECOGNIZING THE GOVERNMENT OF THE CONFEDERATED STATES, restore peace, prosperity, and happiness ; and then try, in an earnest spirit of conciliation and honorable compromise, to regain all that may be practicable. The patriotism and valor of our countrymen has been vindicated ; and where duty has been honorably discharged, no censures can justly rest upon either errors or misfortune.

To conclude, sir, let me repeat that if I am to be forced to lose either, I prefer to save the Constitution of my country at the expense of parting from the seceded States.

" Patria cara, carior Libertas."

I wish, Mr. Speaker, to give notice of and to present the following resolutions which embody the plan of adjustment I intend to propose, and which are substantially the same that I presented at the first called session of this Congress:

Whereas, the deplorable civil war now existing between the States heretofore composing our Union has failed to restore it, and if continued longer will destroy all hope of its restoration in the future, as originally formed and maintained by our Federal Constitution, and no other political union is either desirable or practicable ; and whereas, the interests of humanity, of civilization, and the future of free constitutional government, all concur in requiring that this dreadful contest of arms should be terminated : Therefore,

Be it Resolved, 1. That it is the duty of Congress at once to appoint —— commissioners to effect an armistice between the contending armies, and to secure peace at all events. 2. That said commissioners be empowered, by compromise, to restore the Union if possible ; but if not, then to arrange the terms of a peaceful separation from the Union, as well of those States which now claim to have seceded, as of such others as, by the will of their people in sovereign conventions assembled, may hereafter ordain to secede ; and that said commissioners be solemnly enjoined so to conduct their negotiations as to secure, by every proper and honorable means, if practicable, a more harmonious and permanent reunion of all the States in a commercial, if not a political system. 3. That said commissioners make a report of their transactions to Congress as soon as possible, in order that such legislation may be provided as may be necessary to assemble the people of the several States in convention to determine their action in the premises. 4. That in the event of a refusal by the Government of the United States to secure peace, and the only hopes of a reunion upon the terms and by the means herein provided, or by some other practicable plan, it is hereby recommended to the governments of the several States now composing the Union, at once to take measures to effect these objects.

SPEECH

OF THE

HON. HENRY MAY, OF MARYLAND,

ON THE

BILL TO INDEMNIFY EXECUTIVE TYRANNY,

AND TO CONTINUE IT BY

SUSPENDING THE PRIVILEGE OF THE WRIT OF HABEAS CORPUS,

Delivered in the House of Representatives, February 18th, 1863.

The House having under consideration "An Act to indemnify the President and other persons for suspending the privilege of the writ of *Habeas Corpus*, and acts done in pursuance thereof—"

Mr. MAY said:

MR. SPEAKER,—I do not propose so much to discuss the merits of this bill, as I do to illustrate its evils. I do not mean so much to oppose it, as I do to show its disastrous effects. I know, sir, that the bill which passed this body, and has been returned from the Senate with amendments, will in one of its forms ultimately meet an overwhelming support, and it is therefore in vain for any one to urge objections in the hope of defeating it. There may be a choice proper to be declared now between the two evils; that presented by the bill adopted by the House, and the amendment adopted by the Senate. They are very different in their plan and provisions, but they are designed to accomplish the same thing.

The bill passed by this House is a measure that boldly and quickly, takes up the very foundations of our system of Government. The scheme which has met the approbation of the Senate proposes by a delusive and intricate method, to accomplish the same end. The one is an open and absolute adoption of tyranny, justifying and discharging it from all accountability for its inflictions; the other turns the sufferer over to the courts, and deceiving him, by the hopes of redress, frustrates them all by its artful and arbitrary provisions.

I find, sir, an insurmountable objection at the threshold of inquiry. In my opinion, the Constitution confers upon Congress alone, the power to suspend the privilege of the writ of *habeas corpus*, and only *where* invasion or rebellion exists, and *nowhere* else; and this is a power that cannot for a moment be delegated. The legislative power only can determine when the public safety requires this privilege to be suspended; when, where, how long, and with respect to whom such suspension may be applied. Sir, it is the highest exercise of sovereign power, since the liberty of the citizen is the corner-stone of our system of Government. It was never designed by the founders of our Republic, that this transcendent and tremendous power over the fundamental rights of personal liberty and personal security, should be exercised for an instant of time, by the mere will and discretion of any one man, be he President or not. The genius of our Government forbids it. Its history and precedents, and the opinions of its founders, and statesmen, and jurists, all forbid it.

The bill provides :

> "That during the existence of this rebellion, the President shall be, and is hereby invested with authority to declare the suspension of the privilege of the writ of *habeas corpus*, at such times and in such places, and with regard to such persons as, in his judgment, the public safety may require."

This, sir, in my opinion, erects and commissions despotic power all over the United States.

The House bill is the legitimate product of the ideas of republican liberty held by the dominant party of this House. The Senate's amendment claims to draw a sanction from a Democratic precedent. This amendment, which is, indeed, a substitute for the original bill, claims the example of the celebrated force bill of 1833, to justify it. But, the provisions of this amendment go infinitely beyond the principle asserted by that law.

The force bill adopted in General Jackson's day, proposed simply a transfer of jurisdiction from the State to the Federal courts, in actions brought for some alleged wrong committed in the execution of the revenue laws. The law of 1833 limited the exercise of the right of transferring the case to the period before trial, and there it ceased.

But here, sir, is a proceeding which gives the right to remove a suit in all that comprehensive class of cases brought to redress wrongs committed "under color of any authority derived from, or exercised by, or under the President of the United States," both before trial, and also after judgment. It gives the strange right of an appeal at once from the State to Federal courts: or, if the party shall prefer it, "within six months after judgment by writ of error or other process," to remove the case from a State to the Federal Circuit Court, there "to try and determine the facts and the law, as if the said case had been there originally commenced;" and provided further, "that no such appeal or writ of error shall be allowed where the judgment is in favor of the defendant in the State court," and if "the plaintiff is non-suited, or judgment passed against him, the defendant shall recover double costs." These amendments further provide, that if the Federal judge shall certify that the defendant had probable cause to act, or acted in good faith, then, notwithstanding the jury have found otherwise, and a judgment been recovered by the plaintiff, yet no execution shall issue until after the next ensuing session of Congress ; thus striking down, in effect, the trial by jury in such cases. It is further provided that an appeal shall be allowed the defendant to the Supreme Court of the United States, " whatever may be the amount of the judgment."

Am I not authorized, in view of these unheard-of and most monstrous provisions of a judicial bill, to say that, while proposing to promote justice, it is simply a mean and cunning scheme, designed purposely to frustrate it.

The measure before us, so far from following the principle of the "force bill," flagrantly violates it. That "force bill" simply provided for the impartial administration of law, by allowing, upon certain prescribed conditions, the transfer of jurisdiction. The principle it asserted, *was supremacy of law.* It transferred only such suits as were brought to question the execution of a law. Its language is "for acts done under the revenue laws of the United States, or under color thereof."

But here the alarming principle is asserted of justifying the acts of the Executive committed *against law.* The mere arbitrary will of the President, or his agents, "acting under color of his authority," and despoiling the citizen of his constitutional rights, is now for the first time, to be vindicated and approved by Congress. Congress ought to feel insulted and outraged by such a proposition.

I need hardly add, that I shall vote against these measures.

After the eloquent and exhaustive argument of my friend from Indiana, [Mr. VOORHEES,] there can be no need of further authorities to support the indefeasible title of an American citizen to that blessed writ of *habeas corpus,* which is now to be surrendered.

I beg leave only to add a single reference to that fountain of instruction, the Commentaries of Blackstone, and trust this House may be refreshed by the pure and undefiled principles of civil liberty upon the subject before us, as pronounced by this jurisprudent of a monarchy:

"Of great importance to the public is the preservation of personal liberty, for if once it were left in the power of any, the highest magistrate, to imprison arbitrarily whosoever he or his officers thought proper, there would soon be an end of all other rights and immunities. Some have thought that unjust attacks, even upon life or property, at the arbitrary will of the magistrate, are less dangerous to the Commonwealth than such as are made upon the personal liberty of the subject. To bereave a man of life, or by violence to confiscate his estate without accusation or trial, would be so gross and notorious an act of despotism as must at once convey the alarm of tyranny throughout the whole kingdom; but confinement of the person by secretly hurrying him to jail, where his sufferings are unknown or forgotten, is a less public, a less striking, and therefore a more dangerous engine of arbitrary government; and yet sometimes when the State is in real danger, even this may be a necessary measure. But the happiness of our Constitution is, *that it is not left to the executive power* to determine when the danger of the State is so great as to render this measure expedient; for it is the Parliament only, or legislative power that, when ever it sees proper, can authorize the Crown, by suspending the *habeas corpus* act for a *short and limited time,* to imprison suspected persons without giving any reasons for so doing. But this experiment ought only to be tried in cases of *extreme emergency,* and in these the nation parts with its liberty *for a while* in order to preserve it forever."

I repeat, with emphasis, "for a short and limited period."

Such, is the doctrine of the British constitution. Is ours less free? This bill confers an absolute power on the President, by his own mere will, to suspend the privilege of that great writ, for "such time and in such places, and with regard to such persons as, in his judgment, the public safety may require." Sir, for one, I prefer to enact at once that "Abraham Lincoln rule as all-absolute monarchs rule;" and let him declare his powers in the words:

"Sic volo sic jubeo;
Stat pro ratione voluntas."

Need I remind this House, for an illustration, of the memorable case which occurred in a British court, in which were enunciated the ideas of civil liberty which pervade the jurisprudence of that realm? An humble citizen of a British province, having been 'arrested and imprisoned without trial, by the Governor of that province, sued him for it in England. The defense set up was a sort of divine right, or right of military or judicial power, or all these together, lodged in the office of the Governor, which authorized him to suspend the personal liberty of the subject at his mere will and discretion.

Such was the argument urged before that great judge, Lord Mansfield, who rebuked it at once in the memorable declaration :

"I say that, for many reasons, if this action did not lie against any other man, it shall most emphatically lie against the Governor."

Sir, I commend to the attention of this American House of Representatives, this noble judicial declaration, which throws so tenderly the sanctions of the law around the liberty of the citizen, and especially protects it against the aggressions of supreme power.

Let me add to this another, but not a less glorious instruction. If the oppression of an humble subject gave rise, as history informs us, to the great writ of *habeas corpus* of Charles II., so the oppression of an upright citizen of Maryland,.has produced the noblest exposition of its principles.

Providence seems to have preserved the lengthened life of that illustrious judge who presides over our national judiciary, and to have added fresh vigor to his great intellect and high spirit of independence, that he might vindicate the supremacy of law amid the passions of revolution and the clash of arms.

> "As some tall cliff, that lifts its awful form,
> Swells from the vale, and midway leaves the storm.
> Though round its breast the rolling clouds are spread,
> Eternal sunshine settles on its head."

Sir, it is the pride and consolation of Maryland, in the midst of her afflictions, that she gave both the prisoner and the judge, to make the grandest exposition of the highest right of constitutional government ; and the opinion in the *habeas corpus* case of Merryman will never die, while freedom lives. The spirit of the Constitution presiding in that great judicial declaration, sternly forbids the passage of this bill.

But, Mr. Speaker, I turn now to different thoughts, and will attempt to illustrate the evils of this bill and show the wrongs it practically justifies. I present them with extreme repugnance, and know I cannot expect here to find much approbation of my views. They are addressed rather to my constituents, to my fellow-citizens of Maryland, and to the friends of constitutional liberty. My own pride, and the devotion I ought in this season of their oppression, to cherish for the people of my State, require this declaration. I wish, sir, now that an awakened public sentiment removing restraints and restoring here some freedom of speech, gives the opportunity, for the first time, to say what I think, and give expression to feelings that no caution can make me distrust. I intend to speak with that freedom which is my privilege, and now especially becomes the duties of this place. I do so under the shelter of the Constitution.

To this House alone am I responsible. While I do not invite the infliction of arbitrary power, I solemnly protest against and defy it. Having accepted the office of a Representative, solely in the hope of humbly aiding to preserve peace, and through it our country, when Passion, hurling down the Constitution and the laws, came here to preside, it was then my wish, as I declared on the first day I entered this Hall, to retire from its useless, its hopeless, and mortifying scenes.

I knew that bitter hate, resentment, and jealousy, planted by studied misrepresentation at the North, against Baltimore; and nourished and inflamed by the sinister aims of some of our own unworthy people, would proscribe me as its Representative, unless I proved subservient. The sudden unpremeditated violence of a riot, not unknown to the cities of the North, and to all large cities, was referred to a deep laid conspiracy of a whole people, and their municipal authorities, who bravely and faithfully did all that could be done, to prevent, resist, and overcome it. I but repeat the testimony of the military officers who were assailed, and also of the then Executive of Maryland, who now sits as a Senator in this Capitol. But, sir, I scorn to offer now a defense of Baltimore. The fruitless attempts that I have made to do this in every form of earnest, yet respectful effort—the now prostrate condition of that beautiful, and hospitable city—the abject spirit and degraded situation of its municipal authorities—the utter subjugation of its people, must deny any further attempt of that bitter task to me.

Sir, I prefer, and they whom I represent also prefer, to cast our disgust, contempt, defiance, upon our oppressors. Despising equally the censures or the praises of the prejudiced and the unjust, I disown for my constituents the sympathies of those who, here or elsewhere, have proved indifferent to the brutal oppressions under which the people of Baltimore, and all the manly people of Maryland have suffered ; Maryland, the bright morning star of civil and religious freedom ; the only spot at its settlement where, as your historian, Bancroft, exclaims, " religious liberty found its home, its only home, in the wide world."

The sacred right of suffrage being overthrown in my District, by military power, left me no refuge from the cares and vexations of this place, and I have preferred to suffer the trials and mortifications that I have endured, rather than create a vacancy to be filled by some minion of Executive power, and thus add the bitterest of humiliations to my constituents and to myself.

Sir, it is most unpleasant to dwell upon what may appear to be matters of personal concern, especially at a time when appalling national misfortunes surround us. But it is only from their connection with public liberty, with the principles of constitutional government, that they deserve our notice.

Upon the first day that I took my seat in this Congress, and claimed the privilege of vindicating my conduct from aspersions that newspaper gossip had created about a visit that I undertook, to Richmond, with the knowledge of the President and General Scott, for the sake of peace and our Union, and to soften the horrors of a civil war, and on which a paltry spirit of prying malice had founded a proceeding to expel me from this House, how, sir, was I not treated ? With what rude and clamorous injustice ; and, though supported by the Speaker in the scope of my remarks, I was, by a heavy vote of this House overruling his decision, forced to abandon the attempt. As affecting me personally, that proceeding was insignificant. But, sir, it was a blow struck at the Representative principle, by those who had been created by its breath. How often have I not on every occasion since then, been denied even the privilege of a word of explanation, and that, too, upon subjects relating exclusively to my own constituents?

How often have not my efforts to call attention to the most flagrant and admitted violations of the Constitution and laws, or the most scandalous oppressions against the rights of my constituents and State, under forms of law, been frustrated by ill-disguised malice, objecting in perverted minds? The dominating will of the majority, administering the rules of this House, and trampling into the dust the spirit of parliamentary law and the Constitution, has absolutely, in effect, disfranchised the 4th Congressional District of Maryland.

By indignant speech, by truth-bearing, yet respectful memorials; by resolutions for information, by resolutions to promote investigation, by proposing measures of legislation; by all these means have I earnestly tried to present, inquire into, and redress the most crying oppressions inflicted upon my constituents or fellow-citizens of Maryland. And how have I not approached Executive power by every form of remonstrance, intercession, or appeal, consistent with my own and the dignity of the injured. Invoking the aid of others possessed of influence with the Administration, I have bitterly vexed and mortified my own sensibilities, already too severely tried; and exhausted all the patience and fortitude that nature, adding sympathy to duty, in vain attempted to supply.

Sir, all these efforts have failed, and the single right of voting, with the dignity of silence, (but not submission,) was all that remained to me of the rights, privilege, and influence of a Representative.

Mr. Speaker, Congress had scarcely adjourned its first session, and that Constitutional privilege that protects the presence of its members was no sooner gone, than that other and higher one—for what is the presence of a Representative worth, if free speech be denied?—that provision which gives immunity from accountability elsewhere than to this House, for the legislative actions and conduct of its members, was ruthlessly violated.

The skulking minions of power had gathered around its footstool, and whispering their falsehoods into willing ears, hoped to retrieve the disappointments of ambition, or secure the rewards of a consuming avarice, by denouncing the just, the virtuous, the independent. Informers, spies, and detectives swarming from Washington, with full license against law and liberty, surrounded the outspoken or fearless friend of his country.

Authority, which had meanly prostituted itself to popular clamor, had pledged "the loss of its right arm rather than raise it against a sister State of the South;" had protested with indignant words against the landing of Federal troops to desecrate the soil of the State capital, and "jestingly," it is said, inquired for men of Maryland "to kill Lincoln's men:"—white-livered wretches who were palsied with fear, or who fled at the shadows that popular tumult had cast over Baltimore; aspirants for high stations, or low places, resolved

to obtain them whether by the force of bayonets, or the trickeries of fraud;
contractors, jobbers, and plunderers, assembling together and distorting events
by the aid of a degraded press—a venal and depraved press—that has openly
confessed its shame for having avowed an honest and manly opinion ; mer-
chants, and bankers, and men who had subscribed large sums to provide arms
for the use of our city authorities, at a time of apprehended conflict with the
General Government—these, all together cried out, and echoed back with new
born loyalty, "the Union, the Union, the unconditional Union," and were
forthwith hailed by an alarmed Executive, as the appointed patriots of the
State.

> " Vipers that creep where *man* disdains to climb,
> And having wound their loathscme track
> To the top of this huge mouldering monument of Rome,
> Hang hissing at the nobler man below."

Sir, I do not intend to include in this denunciation those citizens who, with
a genuine patriotism, have sustained the Union, and yet sustain it by military
coercion, however much I differ from their views. I refer only to the selfish,
the malicious, the calculating actors in the sad drama of our subjugation.

Mr. Speaker, even the first in rank among the soldiers of the Republic,
yielded to the base contagion of arbitrary power. He who has won the
triumph of a Northern renown—*but not a victory*—became the partner and the
tool of a conspiracy against the sovereignty of a Commonwealth, ever loyal to
that Constitution which its sages and heroes had so greatly assisted to create and
maintain. By his order, that political ruffian called "military necessity,"
extinguished the legislative power of Maryland, and took captive the liberties
of its best citizens. The destruction of our Legislature by force of arms, was
the grossest act of treason against the guarantees of our Constitutional Government. It was as foul an act of tyranny as was ever committed. The Federal
Government then knew that, so far from intending to pass, or in any way
promote an act of secession, the Legislature had absolutely declined so to do by
its public proceedings. This foulest crime of our century has no pretext to
cover it.

Such, sir, were the hard conditions of a soldier's service in a premeditated
plot to destroy the independence of a border slave-holding State, and which was
first revealed by a ridiculous midnight flight, designed to awaken distrust and
hostility at the North.

The written proofs of this conspiracy exist, and will be produced in better
days, when the parties implicated shall dare to deny them.

The armed agents of the Executive Government, at midnight, invaded my
own home, and the homes of my fellow-citizens, and without any process or
written authority whatever, forcibly arrested and conveyed a large number of
our principal citizens, and State and city officers, to several military bastiles,
under circumstances of restraint and treatment, worse than are visited in civilized
countries upon the most abandoned of convicted malefactors.

I declare that without an accusation, process or examination—nay, sir,
refusing to make a charge, or hear a defence, and with no charge to this hour
alleged, were these unoffending citizens shut up within the walls of a damp, and

filthy casemate—the light of the sun, the open air, and exercise, all these denied—not one among us permitted to cross the threshold of our prison den, where iron bars were added to aid the bayonet of the sentinel, and prevent escape, already impossible, from the triple securities of Fortress Monroe. In vain was the offer of a prisoner's parole for the sake of health within the walls of the fort; in vain, remonstrance. Sir, imagination must supply the disgusting details that made this weary fortnight an imprisonment such as only beasts are subjected to. And will it be credited, when I add, that finally, remonstrance, appealing to the relic of a soldier's pride, brought out the admission from General Wool, that our treatment was so ordered by the Government at Washington.

"O! shame, where is thy blush?"

That depraved nature, which afterwards produced an atrocious order making it a crime to ask for counsel, and denounced prolonged imprisonment as the penalty for claiming this constitutional right, must answer; and the Secretary of State, stand confessed, the author of this glory.

Carried upon an unsafe steamer, then seeking repairs, these prisoners of State, barely escaping the dangers of the autumnal equinox, were thrust among the dreary cells and batteries of Fort Lafayette, crowded together like cattle in the shambles; there for months to be driven from wall to shed, from sunshine to the chilling shade, by the bayonet of the half-civilized imported soldier, until the drum, denying the solace of a poor dim candle, also hushed the voice of social intercourse, and closed the miseries of the day. Then, sir, meditation came to the cot of the victim, and prostrating all his hopes as a citizen, told of the empty glories of that higher aspiration *"Excelsior;"* and darkness, and the sovereignty of the Empire State, together sullenly brooded over the scene of this brutal tyranny. Fort Warren next claimed the custody of these devoted prisoners, and there oppression satiated itself. At length, musing exultingly over the Bay State's boasting motto in the vain words, " *Ense petit placidam sub libertate quietam,*" and having sufficiently honored the great Commonwealths of New York and Massachusetts *as its chosen asylums*, Executive Tyranny suddenly and capriciously released its victims.

Without accusation or defense, without explanation given or received, with nothing but suffering endured by themselves, and those whom nature had bound to them on the one side, and the joys such suffering gave on the other, these citizens of a free constitutional republic, were cast out abruptly from a cruel imprisonment of more than fourteen months' duration.

But, sir, if tyranny was crowned by these transactions in our free United States of America, it found no subjects to concede its realm among those just and fearless men of Maryland. Their spirit, unshaken through all the sufferings they endured, defied the terrors of their persecution. They would have preferred death to bringing any dishonor on their citizenship. Their crime consisted in standing up manfully for the constitutional rights of their State, and the demands of duty· under its laws. Animated by the principles that ever support such a duty in patriotic breasts, they came out of the bastile as free, as proud in spirit, as they had entered it. They attested the integrity and innocence of their actions and thoughts, by spurning every offered concession to power. They could not be forced to sacrifice principle for the sake of personal liberty. It is a proud fact that many of the humblest citizens of Maryland, imprisoned all over the land, under circumstances of the utmost privation and suffering, in camps or common prisons, maintained this noble attitude to the last. And, sir, numbers of them yet maintain it. It is the genuine spirit of American constitutional liberty. The example afforded by their firmness and constancy will go upon the enduring pages of history, and invite the admiration of their countrymen, while eternal infamy awaits those who have oppressed them.

The liberating power of money had soon availed the richest among these prisoners, and a good and fearless citizen, and legislator of our State, against whom the suborned press, and miscreant crew of informers, had clamored as the guiltiest traitor of them all, after a few days confinement, walked from the prison in a mist of gold.

Another, less fortunate in the dispensations of God, had been released that he might stand at the grave of a loved and gallant brother, whose wounds received in the battles of his country, and a long hard service in its navy, had cut short his useful life. In vain, sir, did this prisoner plead for two hours' parole before he was removed from his State, that he might bid the last adieu to this dying brother, and hear from his brave lips the words of love, of blessing, and of fortitude. In vain did this brother's well-earned claims entreat this small boon of the soul's appeal. Communicated to the authorities in Washington, by them it was refused.

Mr. Speaker, that jailor Secretary of State, insensible to this pious duty, with soul abandoned of man and God, waking, perhaps from some debauch, heard that dying appeal only when the fall of the rattling "earth to earth," proclaimed the triumph of his malice; and then mocking with hypocritical compassion the most sacred feelings of the heart, moved by his order the prison to the grave.

Sir, the monuments that patriotism has raised in the congressional cemetery, to mark the ashes of the illustrious Gerry and Clinton, of Pinkney, and of Wirt, were the mute witnesses of this scene, and recognized there in the person of the prisoner, a Representative whose only crime was in trying to preserve the principles of a Government they had so nobly assisted to erect, or maintain. And, although demanded over and over again, to this hour that Secretary has never signified what statue, or even moral obligation, had been, or was even suspected, might be violated. And that prisoner now declares here before the Searcher of all hearts his utter ignorance of any ground for this atrocious tyranny, unless it be found in his public acts as a member of this body.

Sir, when the efforts of a Representative are in this way met and arrested by arbitrary power; when the privileges that are sheltered here by the Constitution are thus wrested away; when reason, argument, and remonstrance are answered by the infliction of a brutal imprisonment; when the earnest, heartfelt pleadings for right, for Constitutional liberty, offered in this place, consecrated to its cause; when the soul-inspired hopes and plans of peace here proposed; when the obligations of that solemn covenant administered by the Speaker's hands are answered:—when all these are answered by the ruthless privation of all

4

privilege, of all peace, of all liberty; and when, alas, this is submitted to by the representatives of the people, and not a voice raised to protest against it, not a whisper of discontent heard here, to this hour, to question it, excepting only in the eloquent effort of my honorable friend from Indiana, (Mr. VOORHEES,) just now delivered, must we not despairingly exclaim, where has the life of our republic gone, where its manhood, where its Constitution, where the spirit of independence that nourished by it, defended it, where the fidelity, the conscience pledged before God to support and protect it? Why, sir, O why have these, the only hopes to keep and bless our future of free government in the surrounding gloom, why have these forsaken us?

Sir, the spirit of Democratic principle cherished in the breasts of the small circle upon this side of the House, was yet too feeble to vindicate the Constitution, thus violated in the person of a member of its party. It was powerless. I repeat that it is most painful to me to present a relation of these personal incidents, which are only deserving of notice from the violence done to my representative character.

Mr. Speaker, usurpation has done its work, and, with a sorrowing breast, I am forced to declare my conviction that the glory of our United States, its incomparable Constitution, is finally destroyed, and a centralized despotism erected upon its ruins—struck through its vitals by that Chief Magistrate, especially elected and sworn before his countrymen at this Capitol, to protect and defend it. And, sir, history will add upon its enduring rolls to the name of Abraham Lincoln, the names also of those representatives of the States and of the people, who have aided this unholy deed. Incapable of comprehending, or not appreciating, and utterly reckless of the priceless principles of our Constitution, the fanaticism of our present rulers has ruined the grandest work of man.

The Legislature of Maryland, and local authorities of Baltimore, were, by brute force of Federal power, crushed out of existence—a legislature that declining in absolute terms to aid any plans of secession, yet, with a noble devotion, asserted its fealty to the Federal Constitution, and by denouncing its invaders, incurred *the guilt of independence;* a city government that having bravely met every responsibility of duty, become criminal only when it persisted *in obeying the laws.* Our right of suffrage was soon destroyed. A base conspiracy of men, holding and disgracing the highest civil and military stations, both at Washington and in our own State, by force of Federal power and a deliberate plan, accomplished this shameful deed. I say, sir, what I do know. The fortunes of war, Mr. Speaker, sometimes make strange revelations, and truth, though crushed by the heel of one soldier, may yet arise by the sword of another.

Sir, the sovereignty of our State thus insulted, outraged and trodden into the dust, Maryland became a subjugated province, and now continues such. Not a single State right, not one constitutional guarantee remaining—not one. A faithless Governor, true only to the miserable influences that appointed him, has surrendered to military power the trusts of the high office he has usurped, and even joined in festive mirth to celebrate the transferred majesty of our laws, and welcome with applauding speech the conquering hero of his fears. The appeals of suffering or pilaged citizens pass by unheeded, and every marauding soldier, with our Governor's assent, now defies the power of the State.

A servile Legislature, whose members, with a few honorable exceptions, were also the mere creatures of military power, hastened by pains and penalties to fasten the yoke upon our people, and laws against fundamental right, believed to have been dictated at Washington, now disgrace our statute-book.

The contented slaves of our people, happy until corrupted in their humble cabin homes, and satisfied under the mild and tolerant spirit that commands their labor, and provides for every want, happier, far happier than the toiling bondman of the Eastern hemisphere, are forced away against their consent, in a defiant and public way by officers of rank, seeking promotion by such merit. Separated from the associations and affections of the master's family, and their own, these poor victims of the blasting civilization of the North, are seduced from slavery only to be cast helpless and friendless upon the chance charity of their deliverers, or the brutal assaults of an affronted soldiery. Sir, the poor children of Africa have been visited by sore afflictions, but this mercy of the Abolitionists is the heaviest of their calamities. And it is so considered by all the intelligent among themselves ; and the future will soon prove how utterly heartless is this miserable speculation upon the destinies of the African race, and, which, if it succeeds, must destroy these poor victims of its blighting care.

Sir, our slaves are enticed into camps or hospitals established all over the State, and there enforced to remain by "military protection," directed by the Federal Executive, until they are transported beyond the State, to complete this scandalous scheme of larceny.

Fugitive slaves arrested here in this District, created by the design of recent legislation, as a refuge against the obligation of the supreme law, are no sooner committed by judicial authority to await the demand of the owner under the guarantees of the Constitution, than armed soldiers of the provost guard, by force, release and set them free. The musket has taken the place of the deed of manumission. In vain has the marshal, the friend and daily companion of the President, remonstrated against such lawlessness. Sir, this base and fraudulent scheme of robbing the people of Maryland of their property, yet goes on.

The negro slave is indeed, in some respects, the only free man in Maryland ; for while military surveillance inspects the social visits of the master, and a pass alone gives him the privilege of the highway, the slave goes freely, and is aided on his way.

Restrictions on our internal trade and commerce, in palpable violation of the Constitution and repeated decisions of the Supreme Court, are established by the Department of the Treasury, and a delegated discretion to understrappers in our custom houses has inflicted and yet maintains most vexatious, burden-some, and expensive conditions upon our people. Rigorous rules that press upon an entire population are made a pretext to screen the worthless vigilance that ought to guard the lines that separate contending armies. Sir, as they are not imposed in the exercise of any military power, we must conclude they are designed simply to oppress us.

Boards of Trade, (unknown to law,) created of petty politicians, search the breasts of every man and woman, and by oaths and fees harrass each household in its demands for food or clothing, or other necessaries of life, only to be obtained in Baltimore, thus assailing its prosperity and discriminating in favor of other ports and places. And even the sacred liberty of conscience is proscribed at its very birthplace on our continent, and the Catholic citizen of Maryland by "Know-Nothing" officials required "to swear over the sign of the cross," after taking the usual oath on the Holy Evangely. I have, sir, already offered to submit the conclusive evidence of this fact to a committee of this House. It cannot with truth be denied.

Our private papers have been forcibly seized and brought to Washington, and are yet detained in the State Department. Property of all kinds is seized, and carried off openly and habitually by agents of the Federal Government, or its marauding troops, and confiscations, mocking judicial authority, are pronounced by the captors themselves. In vain does the owner demand either compensation or security, or, often times, even the evidence of a receipt for it. I am now, sir, referring to seizures of the property of our citizens at their homes, and without a pretext alleged for seizing it.

Mr. Speaker, the property of our citizens has been seized under these circumstances and brought here to Washington, and after considerable portions of it had been appropriated by the agents of the United States, the residue delivered up to the owner upon payment of heavy sums as ransoms, by order of the then military governor here, one General Wadsworth. With no evidence to seize, or hold, or condemn the property after being thus pillaged, it is, at the expense of a heavy transportation to the owner, returned to him upon the payment of a sum of money; and this, with a full knowledge, by this governor, of all the facts; and to crown this outrage, the owner was subjected to a long imprisonment in the Old Capitol prison, simply for stating these things.

Sir, not only are property and liberty thus outraged, but the securities of home are habitually invaded, and alarm carried into the bosoms of our wives and children, by the rude and violent conduct of undisciplined soldiers. I am able to state instances where such brutal visits have destroyed the lives of helpless women, or paralized them by premeditated alarms. What has been my own case will serve to illustrate hundreds of others more aggravated, and of frequent occurrence.

But a few days before this session of Congress begun, a vulgar ruffian, who holds the title of provost marshal of Talbot county, during my absence, with a troop of dragoons visited my country home, and planting men with weapons drawn around the house, without warrant or order, or any process, proceeded to search and open every place and portion of my premises, breaking locks and doors, and desecrating every privacy of home. Neither the situation of defenceless wife and children, nor those prescriptive guards that create the castle of the home, nor the sacred injunctions of a Constitution that forbids such searches, could restrain the unlicensed powers emanating from the Secretary of War. Sir, under his general order, as it was alleged, a small pistol that another and younger brother who now sleeps in his grave, had carried fighting the enemies of his country through the war with Mexico, and that came to me as a memento of him, was seized and carried away as a trophy of this exploit, or proof of a magazine that had made my residence so terrible a place.

Sir, that search was designed as an outrage, as a menace. The miserable tool who committed it, after closing all places where stimulus was sold within the county, was soon convicted by military authority of selling, with his own hands, behind the counter of a low tavern, kept by himself, whisky to soldiers, and, I believe, to negroes. Nevertheless, he remains a provost marshal of the War Department, with despotic powers. Such are the emanations of Federal authority, which have displaced our State judiciary, and now dominate over our people. Free speech, a free press—those boasts of American liberty—are prostrate in the dust. But, sir, the swaggering minions of power are licensed to speak, to print what they please, and scurrilous newspapers are even bold enough to attempt to command the action of this House against its members. The house of God, even, is invaded by military power, and the flag of our country, the symbol of civil and religious freedom, gains its first victory over the sacred rights of conscience in the hands of a Federal General in Baltimore, and a faithful minister of God is arrested and imprisoned for defending these, his inalienable rights. And even women and little children are arrested and oppressed for showing gaudy ribbons so shocking to the sensitive imaginations of a prurient loyalty. And, sir, how shall I describe the taunts, the insults, the threats, the violence, that have assailed the pride, the dignity, the helpless spirit, of our down-trodden men and women and children of Maryland. Words cannot attempt it.

Mr. BINGHAM. I desire to ask the gentleman from Maryland a question.

Mr. MAY. I yield, with pleasure, to the gentleman from Ohio.

Mr. BINGHAM. I desire to know from the gentleman to what minister he refers ?

Mr. MAY. I allude to the Rev. Mr. Dashiel, of the Methodist Episcopal church.

Mr. BINGHAM. When was he arrested ?

Mr. MAY. A few days ago.

Mr. BINGHAM. I desire to know from the gentleman from Maryland what this minister was arrested for?

Mr. MAY. He was arrested because he dared to remove from his own church, from his own property, where a religious society has been in the habit of worshipping God, a flag which had been surreptitiously placed there in the night by some evil-minded person.

Mr. BINGHAM. Was it the flag of the United States ?

Mr. MAY. It was the flag of the United States.

Mr. BINGHAM. Does the gentleman pretend that the minister owned the church ?

Mr. MAY. I affirm that fact. He has either a lease of the property or it belongs to him absolutely. It is a place where he has instructed youth during the week, and led his congregation to worship God on the Sabbath.

Mr. Speaker, I have no patience for this sort of vain flourishing of flags here. I am sick of it. I do not respect our national flag when it is planted in opposition to those divine rights of which it is a high and glorious emblem. When high advanced, sir, in the service of our country's Constitution, and to maintain its laws, it shall ever win from me the applause of my heart's heart. But when any man dares, intoxicated with notions of military power, to set up a gross tyranny in this free land, and takes that emblem to strike the sacred rights of conscience, he shall be denounced by me, although the victim of his oppression may be the humblest of my fellow-citizens.

I feel authorized, sir, to speak as I do in this case. This faithful and upright minister of the Gospel is my constituent; and I am acquainted with the circumstances of the case.

The gentleman from Ohio [Mr. Bingham] will find, if he takes the trouble of investigating the facts of the case, that the account I have given is correct. I have been prepared with a resolution of inquiry about this affair, and tried to offer it; and if I have an opportunity of doing so, and it be adopted, I will undertake to prove before the Committee on the Judiciary, of which the gentleman and myself are members, the facts which I relate.

Mr. Speaker, is it because we have been too weak to resist these oppressions, that we have been forced to submit to them? Sir, we are oppressed because we are defenceless.

Does a Marylander hear the recital of that infernal outrage that dragged from the bench where he was presiding, an honored and fearless judge, and, attempting his life, scattered his blood over the ermine of justice, and laid him insensible upon the floor, simply because he openly declared his respect for and claimed obedience to the Constitution? Does any true-hearted American know that such brutality was approved and justified by a cruel and prolonged imprisonment of that judge, inflicted by order of the Executive, with a full knowledge of the facts, and that such a wrong is yet unredressed—nay, sir, yet approved, justified, praised—and the ruffians who inflicted it are now revelling amidst the ruins of our laws and liberties, with superadded authority and force, emanating from Washington?

Sir, I repeat—does any Marylander, does any man of America, hear these things, and not feel that God-inspired instinct of resistless power awakened in free hearts, that ever hath crushed despotism, and ever will?

Mr. Speaker, after this recital, let me be justified by simply repeating what is written in the Constitution, article fourth of the amendments:

"The right of the people, to be secure in their persons, houses, papers, and effects, against unreasonable searches and seizures, shall not be violated, and no warrant shall issue but upon probable cause, supported by oath or affirmation, and particularly describing the place to be searched and the person or things to be seized."

Sir, what efforts have I not made with every circumstance of respect for the dignity and rules of this House, and in every form of application attempted to gain a consideration of these heavy, insupportable grievances of Maryland; and what single one has received even the cold ceremony of a reception? Not one! But all rejected with insulting haste, or "laid upon the table," to rest there forever.

Maryland is treated here, too, as a subjugated province. Stripped of every attribute of her sovereignty, a caucus of revolutionary fanatics has appointed our rulers, and Ohio and Illinois furnished the pro-consuls of our conquered State, Mr. Bingham and Lovejoy. If the Federal Constitution had guaranteed to Maryland the curse of a despotism, instead of a "Republican form of government," its duty in this respect could not have been more faithfully kept.

But, surrounded as she is by misfortunes, it is now, and shall continue to be the glory of Maryland, that her prostrate constitution and laws, her subjugated people attest their spirit and patriotism, in meeting and defying the encroachments of arbitrary power, that they were too feeble by force to oppose. With true republican pride, her citizens can repeat her noble declaration of rights, that " the doctrine of non-resistance to arbitrary power, is absurd, slavish, and destructive to the peace and happiness of mankind." And, repeating it, appeal to Heaven as witness, that its precious injunction has been faithfully kept, and yet abides firmly in their hearts ; and I must, sir, in a spirit of admonition, now and here declare my conviction, that the people of Maryland will and ought, by arms, to defend their constitutional rights, if longer trampled on ; and let the bloodshed rest on the souls of the aggressors, or the authority that encourages or permits their lawlessness.

Mr. Speaker, Maryland, though now prostrate, will again rise. When passion and brute force shall have passed away, or be driven from her soil, and the benign genius of free government returns again to preside over her destinies ; then, her own people, if united and organized, will be able themselves to determine her lot. Let them be assured of this, and also be prepared. And then, also, comes a retribution. And while we may hope that her faithless children, who have stood indifferent to her fate, may be forgiven ; yet, sir, they must not be forgotten ; but those self-abasing wretches who, with parricidal hands, have helped to strike their own State's sovereignty down, shall rest in the full assurance of that day of account that must come, in the sure providence of God. And, sir, instructed by the language of the present Secretary of State, addressed to my constituents, in a lecture delivered by him on the 22d of December, 1848, "if a separation from the Union shall ever be necessary, let us hope that long habits of discipline and mutual affection, may enable the American people to add another and final lesson on the excellence of Republics—*that of dividing without violence, and re-constructing without the loss of liberty.*" Heaven grant that such may be the happy destiny of Maryland.

Mr. Speaker, could I be persuaded to believe that any friend of the Constitution would impute these views to feelings of a personal resentment, it would inflict upon me inexpressible pain. And, sir, could I hear that any pure-minded and pure-hearted citizen of my State—

" A brave man struggling in the storms of fate,—
And greatly falling with a falling State,"—

could justly accuse me of a failure to meet the sternest demands of duty, in this crisis of our national calamity, I should go, sir, to my final accountability with an embittered life.

Amidst the cares and perplexities, the anxieties and excitements, that in this unhappy season of national trial have surrounded the duties of public life, we may have erred in finding or in following them. But if a disinterested love of country ; if self-denial and a devotion to the duties of the Constitution and welfare of our fellow-citizens ; if a readiness to incur responsibility, except that which provokes oppression, without the means to resist or redress it; if a judgment that hesitates to defy reckless power, only to inflict or prolong its sufferings upon others; if that sense of public accountability that cares for the many while sympathizing with the few, and refuses, at the demand of any, to resign the trust for all; if a spirit of moderation and conciliation, putting aside resentment, and presiding over all passion for the sake of peace, of human life, for free government, for the future of civil liberty; if, sir, these aims and motives, preserving and seeking the opportunities that public confidence has bestowed to do all *practicable good*, if these cannot support and protect a representative, and preserve his name from reproach, then, sir, not only has the Constitution failed, but man, the citizen, has also failed.

The present prostrate condition of Maryland, and the alienation of her people, has been caused entirely by the lawless policy pursued by the Federal Government, and its unscrupulous agents.

Not a solitary act against law, or their Federal relations, can be justly imputed to their State authorities or to them. After an experience of two years, not one of our citizens has been even tried for such an offence. But if such acts have been committed, the courts of the United States have never been obstructed in our State. Supported by the military power, the Federal judiciary was never so strong before in Maryland. The district attorney and marshal, selected by the President, and the latter possessing the exclusive discretion to select both the grand and petit juries, the whole power of both preventive and punitive justice was to be found in the jurisdiction of these courts.

Sir, no plea of a military necessity at any time, for a moment, could be proved in Maryland. A zealous Governor supporting the Federal power, and a supple Legislature, added together the powers of both State and Federal Governments. Was not here sufficient strength to arrest and punish the citizen according to law? Has it ever been pretended that any organization existed to resist law? Sir, not one honest or true man lives in Maryland, or any where, who is not forced to believe that the oppressions of our people have been as reckless and unjustifiable, as they were cruel and cowardly.

Maryland has even been praised in reports of Secretarys, and a proclamation of the President, for the loyalty of her people, and the protection of the Constitution promised as a reward of her fealty. And yet, sir, we perceive how delusive is this new pledge. Why are the scandalous invasions, the aggressions, the restrictions, the insults, the oppressions upon our plainest rights, yet continued? Why these arrests made, why imprisonments prolonged, property seized and confiscated, commerce interdicted, our slaves removed? Is it even pretended by those who commit them, that there now exists a military necessity, or any necessity, to justify these proceedings?

Our people have been forced to associate tyranny with the exercise of Federal power. They see nothing but injustice and wrong in its acts. They believe them to be wanton, and inflicted on grounds of a personal, political, or sectional influence. They know they are unnecessary, and could easily be restrained or prevented, and are not.

Sir, we are not ignorant that allegiance and protection are mutual and reciprocal rights; and as a people fit to be free, ever should, we feel that the course of oppression inflicted upon us by the Federal Government must, if persisted in, finally absolve us from any legal or moral allegiance to it.

It is useless to deny that the people of Maryland have become alienated from the Government by the acts of Executive power. If, sir, they are to be continued, we see nothing but calamity in the future of the Federal Government—nothing but oppression in maintaining polical relations with it. The hopes of civil liberty now beckon us away.

A centralized Federal system absorbing the States is now before our eyes. We see the movement of its giant limbs in the schemes of the measure now under consideration, in the plan of a national bank system, and a national guard, the conscription bill and other alarming measures. We, in Maryland, have long felt its presence in the omnipotence of Executive power.

The source of our political system, a free ballot-box, has been crushed by the heel of the soldier, and our freedom of speech, our liberty of the press, our private property, our personal liberty, our personal security, all these fundamental rights of man are overthrown. And what has been the experience of the past may be the fate of our future. The divine right of a refuge from intolerable oppression is the common heritage of all mankind. Let no one misunderstand me. I speak here only for constitutional right, and for its sake alone declare, with candor, my humble views of our future. With the Constitutions, both Federal and State, as my guides, and ever profoundly anxious to preserve the blessings of law and of peace within our borders, I have earnestly tried, against both personal and political ties and associations, to support constituted authority for the sake of State sovereignty, believing from our position, that the people of Maryland could only walk safely through the fires of this dreadful revolution under its authority firmly and conscientiously administered. And while I have praised the spirit of loyalty of the Legislature that met at Frederick, (I mean, sir, the only loyalty that I respect, *loyalty to the Constitution*,) so I have sternly condemned what at the time seemed to be, or were represented as its tendencies, either to establish arbitrary State power on the one hand, or to excite a sanguinary and fruitless revolution on the other. Sir, no man in Maryland has, under circumstances of greater political or personal responsibility than myself, maintained the cause of the Union. No man in America would now make a more devoted sacrifice to restore it to its pristine harmony, if that were practicable. But alas, sir, it is not.

With all the love that I have been accustomed to regard our Union, for its past blessings to ourselves, and for the hopes that it has inspired for the regeneration of mankind, I must yet declare that our CONSTITUTION has been the only source of these blessings and these hopes. If it be lost, let the Union, then an empty sound die away and be forgotten. Take from me, sir, the Constitution, and I will try by revolution and the help of God, to save at least the eternal principles of civil liberty which His providence has bestowed.

APPENDIX.

As Mr. MAY's colleagues, Messrs. THOMAS and LEARY, who replied to his speech, declined to allow him the opportunity of correcting what he declared to be their mis-representations—and the House of Representatives, following such example, also refused to allow Mr. MAY to be heard in reply after they had concluded, and when Mr. WICKLIFFE had yielded the floor to him for this purpose; and such refusal was a violation of the uniform practice of the House—the following proofs are offered to vindicate truth and to show that his constituents are opposed to, and elected Mr. MAY *to oppose coercion.*

The subjoined extracts from Mr. MAY's letter of the 5th of June, 1861, continually published before his election, shows the basis on which he became a candidate and was elected to Congress as *an opponent of military coercion,* any statements to the contrary notwithstanding:

"I profess an unconditional reverence for and obedience to the principles and authority of our Federal Constitution, which, having created our Union of States, is alone competent to maintain it.

"For my reply to your first question I must be allowed to repeat the following, quoted from my letter (public) of the 14th May, authorizing my nomination :

"'By a compromise, amending our Constitution, I can yet see *the paths of peace,* which, with the favor of Heaven, I intend always to point out to my countrymen and *for myself most faithfully to follow them.*' The geographical position of Maryland requires her Representatives to hold the olive branch rather than the sword, and this is her honor as well as her interest. We ought upon this point to be a united people.

"I have ever sternly opposed the platform of principles and hostile policy of the Republican party, and ever will, with an uncompromising spirit, believing it to be a sectional and aggressive party.

"Do not these explicit declarations place me on *the side of peace and compromise, and against those who prefer military coercion and a desolating war ?*

"Being unable to perceive any error or obscurity in this statement of my position, I can see no reason to alter it."

So much for the assertion that Mr. MAY's votes against war measures excited surprise.

The basis upon which Messrs. THOMAS and LEARY rested their speeches, the security of suffrage, and the prevailing peace, order, and contentment of our people is so notoriously unfounded as not to require evidence to disprove it. If Mr. MAY had been heard, he was prepared with conclusive evidence on these points. It has, how-ever, been elsewhere furnished, and, as stated in his speech, the whole scheme of a bold conspiracy to destroy our suffrage will be exposed at a future day in proofs that no one can even question. The quiet of Maryland "is the quiet of despotism."

It is a sufficient commentary on these speeches simply to say that the day after their delivery a distinguished public man (Mr. VALLANDIGHAM) was prevented by the open menaces of mob-violence from delivering a lecture in Baltimore "on the literature of the Bible," for the sake of charity, and the military authority governing Baltimore, failed to satisfy the managers of the lecture of its disposition to protect him.

And to add another illustration, the principal independent journal of Baltimore has been prevented from publishing Mr. MAY's speech, through fear of being suppressed, while the replies to it of Messrs. THOMAS and LEARY have been published in full in the newspapers supporting the Administration.

The following, copied from the Congressional Globe, (the official report of the transactions of Congress,) will serve to illustrate the oppressions of Maryland and show the dispositions of the popular branch of Congress, and may aid the future his-torian of Maryland :

EXTRACTS FROM MR. MAY'S SPEECH "ON THE OPPRESSIONS OF MARYLAND."

An effort having been made to expel Mr. MAY from the House of Representatives, immediately upon taking his seat in the present Congress, on the 18th July, 1861, in an indignant speech, among other things, he said :

Mr. MAY. I am more than gratified, sir, that the Judiciary Committee have, in this decisive way, condemned an unparalleled outrage on the privileges of a Representative ; and that, on an investigation, those who prompted it here, being called before the committee to adduce their proofs, retired from the accusation, and have admitted that there were no grounds for it—not a shadow of evidence to sustain it.

What am I to say of a proceeding like this—based, as the report itself confesses it to have been, upon mere newspaper rumor? Upon the idle gossip of the hour, a Representative of the people is to be arraigned for a grave, nay, a heinous offence, and the attempt made to strip him of his right to a seat upon this floor. I have no words to express my indignation and disgust at this proceeding.

    *   *   *   *   *   *   *   *   *   *   *

For myself, let me say, that as it affected me personally, the issue was of the lightest consequence. At the time I received notice of this accusation, it was under my consideration whether I could with honor come here and enter upon the duties of a Representative upon this floor. The humiliation that I felt at the condition of my constituents, bound in chains; absolutely without the rights of a free people in this land; every precious right belonging to them under the Constitution, prostrated and trampled in the dust; military arrests in the dead hour of the night; dragging the most honorable and virtuous citizens from their beds, and confining them in forts; searches and seizures the most rigorous and unwarrantable, without pretext of justification; that precious and priceless writ of *habeas corpus*, for which, from the beginning of free government, the greatest and best of men have lived and died—all these prostrated in the dust; and hopeless imprisonment inflicted without accusation, without inquiry or investigation, or the prospect of a trial. Sir, is there a Representative of the people of the United States here in this body, acknowledging the sympathy due to popular rights and constitutional liberty, who does not feel indignant at the perpetration of these outrages? If so, it will be the opportunity of this House promptly to redress them. The country will see whether that redress will be afforded; we shall see whether there is not yet a redeeming spirit in our Constitution, that amid the fierce conflict of arms will yet appear like an angel of peace in this Hall, dedicated to republican freedom, to vindicate the majesty of the violated laws.   *   *   *

Mr. MAY. Mr. Speaker, I have spoken of some considerations looking to my presence as a Representative in this Hall. I was about to say that, in view of my own dignity, if I had alone consulted it, my own sense of the privileges and the responsibilities of a Representative here. and of my own judgment upon the transactions of this body, and the circumstances of my situation as a Representative, I should have absolutely declined to take the oath of office here, and resigned the empty honor of my seat. I would have preferred to wait and see whether the action of this body would have stricken off the chains from my constituents, and restored them fully to all their constitutional privileges.   *   *   *   *   *   *   *   *

But I am speaking also in the spirit of a citizen who owes obligations higher than these—that highest of duties which binds him to maintain the Constitution of his country. And speaking in this spirit, and under the shelter of its authority and majesty, neither by my silence nor consent shall one of its precious principles ever be stricken down, even in the person of the humblest of my constituents or my countrymen.

  *   *   *   *   *   *   *   *   *   *   *

I complain, Mr. Speaker, of these outrages and oppressions. I denounce them as unparalleled in the history of free government; and I call upon the Representatives of the people, *if they have the manhood and spirit worthy of their country*, to emancipate the down-trodden people of Baltimore from the military tyranny under which they are now groaning, and which has so utterly prostrated their constitutional liberties.

Mr. STEVENS. I move, as the sense of this House, that the gentleman is not in order. I believe it is the sense of this House that the gentleman is not in order.

The SPEAKER. The gentleman from Maryland is entitled to the floor.

Mr. STEVENS. I submit the motion, that it is the sense of this House, that the gentleman is not in order ; and I ask the Chair to put that motion to the House.

Mr. VALLANDIGHAM. I rise to a question of order. No such motion can be entertained while the gentleman is upon the floor.

The SPEAKER. The Chair cannot entertain the motion of the gentleman from Pennsylvania. The Chair has decided that he cannot determine for the gentleman from Maryland what is a personal explanation. If the gentleman is not satisfied with that decision he can take an appeal from the decision of the Chair.

Mr. STEVENS. I take an appeal from the decision of the Chair.

Mr. VALLANDIGHAM. I move to lay the appeal on the table, and call for the yeas and nays on the motion.

The yeas and nays were ordered.

The question was taken; and it was decided in the negative—yeas 53, nays 82.

So Mr. MAY was ruled out of order and compelled to take his seat.

Mr. DAWES then moved that Mr. MAY be allowed to proceed "*in order.*"

* * * * * *

Mr. MAY. Sir, I must absolutely decline further to proceed. if I am to be subject to this sort of interruption and restriction. I will go no further now, and must trust to the chances of an opportunity, and of being sufficiently restored to health, when the field of debate may be opened wide enough to allow me to speak my sentiments with the freedom that becomes me, and the rights of my constituents. I shall proceed no further in my remarks now, but content myself with the presentation of this memorial, and the request that it be referred to the Committee on the Judiciary, and be printed.

It is a memorial from the House of Representatives from the Police Commissioners of Baltimore, upon a subject most vital to the liberties of the people of the United States. It is couched in clear and candid language, and presents both sides of the question. Full justice is done to the military authorities of the United States, who have inflicted what I consider a most unparalleled oppression. While the memorial is expressed in language respectful to the House, it is at the same time the language of independence, and comes to us in the spirit of citizens fully conscious of their constitutional rights, and resolved to claim them here. * * * * * * *

Being questioned by Mr. COLFAX, of Indiana, as to a conspiracy in Maryland, Mr. MAY replied—

That there are thirty-thousand men—ay, and more—who, unless the heel of oppression is lifted from them, will, if they can get the opportunity, vindicate their constitutional rights and liberties, is absolutely true. *I proclaim it here to-day; and I will be one of the number of them, on grounds of constitutional right, and to resist tyranny and oppression*—on grounds of American right—on grounds of consecrated and defined legal right. These are the grounds on which it stands. As for a conspiracy against the United States, having for its object any attempt against the Government, or the overthrow of the military authorities, the statement is absolutely preposterous. It does not now exist. It never did exist. I tell the gentleman from Indiana it never did exist. It rests upon the relation of spies and informers—those detestable miscreants, who, from the beginning of the world, have been held in scorn and contempt by all honest men. Because of their imaginings and malicious falsehoods, founded upon the most malignant motives, a loyal people—a vast majority of whom are true to their duty to the Constitution of the country—are dominated over in this way, and placed under the heel of military power. I denounce the whole of it as rank, gross, unparalleled oppression. That is my answer to the gentleman from Indiana.

Now, a few words in reference to the residue of that article. I have nothing to reserve. What I may do, and what I have done in this business of our unhappy national troubles is as open as the light of day. I invite the scrutiny of my countrymen upon every action of my life, and every thought in connection with our unhappy discord. Elected a Representative by the people who conferred upon me this honor by a large majority—elected upon the basis of peace, conciliation and compromise, as the only means of saving this great, prosperous and happy Government and country of ours, I stand committed to these measures ; and, sir, with my life I intend to promote them, come what may come. Springing from a love of peace, and for the sake of my countrymen, with a heart alive to those fraternal interests that ought to be dearest to us all, in trying to assuage those horrible calamities now impending over us, and with the hope of bringing us together once more as a happy and united people, I will go anywhere, everywhere ; I say, sir, I will lay down my life for this result cheerfully. Elected upon such a platform, to serve such high and holy objects—appealing to the heart, conscience and every future accountability—I stand firm and unshaken in my convictions, and all the menaces, all the frowns, and the dominations of all the powers of earth cannot move me from my love of peace, and devotion, through it, to the safety of my country. Here is where I stand, and here I mean through the future to stand.

* * * * * * *

I wish to admit that everywhere where I have gone, I have spoken the language of denunciation of tyranny, and I mean to do it everywhere.

40

ARREST OF THE POLICE COMMISSIONERS OF BALTIMORE.

On the 24th of July, 1861, Mr. MAY presented, through the Judiciary Committee, this resolution of inquiry :

"*Resolved*, That the President be requested immediately to communicate to this House (if in his judgment not incompatible with the public interests,) the grounds, reasons, and evidence, upon which the Police Commissioners of Baltimore were arrested, and are now detained as prisoners at Fort McHenry."

NOTE.—The words in parenthesis were introduced by the Committee, and were the means of passing the resolution.

To which on the 30th of July, 1861, the President returned as follows :

The SPEAKER laid before the House a message from the President of the United States, in response to the resolution of the House of the 24th instant, asking the grounds, reasons, and evidence, upon which the Police Commissioners of Baltimore were arrested, and are now detained prisoners at Fort McHenry, stating that it is judged to be incompatible with the public interest to furnish said information ; which was laid on the table, and ordered to be printed.

POLICE COMMISSIONERS OF BALTIMORE.

On the 31st July, 1861, Mr. MAY offered the following resolution :

WHEREAS, the Constitution of the United States declares that no warrant shall issue but upon probable cause, supported by oath or affirmation; that no citizen shall be deprived of his liberty without due process of law ; and that the accused shall enjoy the right of a speedy trial by a jury of the district where the offense was committed : and whereas Charles Howard, William H. Gatchell, and John W. Davis, citizens of Baltimore, in the State of Maryland, were, on the 1st day of July, 1861, seized without warrant. and without any process of law whatever, by a body of soldiers of the Army of the United States, by order of Major General Banks, alleged to have been made in pursuance of orders issued from the Headquarters of the Army at Washington, and were removed by force, and against their will, from their homes to Fort McHenry, where they have since been confined as prisoners ; and whereas the said military officer, without warrant or authority of law, superseded and suspended the official functions of the said Charles Howard and others, members of the Board of Police of Baltimore ; and whereas, since their said arrest, a grand jury attending the United States District Court, in Baltimore, and selected and summoned by a marshal appointed by the present Executive of the United States, having jurisdiction in the premises, and having fully investigated all cases of alleged violation of law, has finally adjourned its session without finding any presentment or indictment, or other proceeding, against them, or either of them ; and the President of the United States, being requested by a resolution of the House of Representatives to communicate the grounds, reasons, and evidence for their arrest and imprisonment, has declined so to do, because he is advised that it is incompatible with the public interests; and whereas, since these proceedings, the said citizens, with others, have been. by force and against their wills, transferred by the authority of the Government of the United States beyond the State of Maryland and the jurisdiction of that court which it is their constitutional right to claim, and are to be subjected to an indefinite, a hopeless, and cruel imprisonment in sor. e fort or military place, unfit for the confinement of the citizen, at a remote distance from their families and friends, and this without any accusation, investigation or trial whatever ; and whereas the constitutional privilege of the writ of *habeas corpus* has been treated with contempt, and a military officer (the predecessor of General Banks) has taken upon himself the responsibility of wilful disobedience to the writ, and the privilege of the same now continues suspended, thereby subordinating the civil to the military power, thus violating and overthrowing the Constitution of the United States, and setting up in its stead a military despotism ; and whereas the Congress of the United States regards the acts aforesaid as clear and palpable violations of the Constitution of the United States, and destructive to the liberties of a free people : Therefore :

Resolved, That the arrest and imprisonment of Charles Howard, William H. Gatchell, and John W. Davis, and others, without warrant and process of law, is flagrantly unconstitutional and illegal ; and they should, without delay, be released, or their case remitted to the proper judicial tribunals, to be lawfully heard and determined.

Mr. HUTCHINS. I move to lay the resolution on the table.

Mr. BINGHAM. I raise the question of order that the resolution is not admissable under the standing order of the House.

The SPEAKER. The gentleman from Ohio raises the question of order, that under the standing order by which the House is confined to the consideration of bills and resolutions relating to military and naval operations, and financial questions relating thereto, and judicial questions of a general character, the resolution is not in order.

Mr. MAY. Does not that resolution relate to the operations of the Army of the United States? Is it not an allegation of the tyranny practiced under color of military authority?

The SPEAKER. The Chair does not think that such declarations on the part of the House have anything to do with the military operations of the Government.

Mr. MAY. Is it the decision of the Chair that the point of order is well taken?

The SPEAKER. The Chair so decides.

Mr. MAY. Well, I appeal from that decision.

Mr. BINGHAM. I move to lay the appeal upon the table.

Mr. STEVENS. There is another ground on which that paper is not in order. It is not in order to make a speech at this time; and that is nothing but a speech.

The resolution was then ruled out.

PROSCRIPTION OF REPRESENTATION.

On the 24th July, 1861, Mr. STEVENS, of Pennsylvania, presented and was discussing a bill relating *exclusively* to Baltimore, Mr. MAY, having failed to get the floor, interrupted Mr. S. as follows:

Mr. STEVENS. I have only to say that this bill provides for the payment of the police established in the city of Baltimore by the commanding general of that division, and there is no other fund out of which they can be paid; the State of Maryland having made no provision.

Mr. MAY. Will the member from Pennsylvania allow me to say a word or two?

Mr. STEVENS. To ask a question.

Mr. MAY. I will limit my observations strictly to the consideration of the question.

Mr. STEVENS. Oh no; I do not yield for observations.

Mr. MAY. I am the Representative of Baltimore.

The SPEAKER. The gentleman from Pennsylvania declines to yield.

Mr. MAY. I hope he will allow me to be heard upon this question.

Mr. STEVENS. I have already granted too large an indulgence for debate.

Mr. MAY. Then I can only protest, as I do solemnly, against the bill. It is a bill to provide the wages of oppression.

The SPEAKER. The gentleman from Maryland is not in order.

FUGITIVE SLAVES FROM MARYLAND.

Mr. MAY. I offer the following resolution, and demand the previous question upon it:

WHEREAS, Maryland has been proclaimed by the President of the United States to be a loyal State, and its people are entitled to the benefits and protection of the Constitution and laws of the United States. And whereas, "persons held to service and labor" in the said State, "under the laws thereof," and escaping therefrom into the District of Columbia, have been therein arrested, and after due examination by the commissioners appointed by law for that purpose, have been committed to prison within said District in order that they may be delivered up "on the claim of the party to whom their service and labor may be due," according to the provisions of the Constitution of the United States. And whereas, before the opportunity has been afforded to said parties to make such claim, and immediately after the said arrest and detention, military officers, acting under the authority of the military governor or provost marshal of said District, or both, have, in many cases of such detention, demanded from the marshal of said District having such persons in custody, their release, and this without any legal warrant or process of any kind; and upon the refusal of said marshal to deliver up said persons, have, with armed bodies of soldiers, forcibly released said persons, from custody as aforesaid, and, in effect, discharged them altogether from said service and labor, and any future reclamation of the same by the parties to whom it is due, to the destruction of their rights of property and of the solemnly guarantied rights of the people of Maryland, and in palpable violation of the Constitution and laws of the United States: Therefore,

Be it Resolved, 1. That the Committee on the Judiciary be instructed to investigate the facts and law concerning the premises, and to report the result of their investigation at an early day, together with such measures of legislation, as may, in the judgment of the committee, be necessary to put an end to such lawless and unconstitutional proceedings.

2. That a copy of this preamble and resolutions be transmitted to the President of the United States, and that he be requested to see that the Constitution and laws be faithfully executed here, in this District, so immediately under his personal observation and official authority.

Mr. LOVEJOY. Will the gentleman from Maryland allow me to suggest an amendment?

Mr. MAY. I object.

The previous question was seconded, and the main question ordered.

Mr. S. C. FESSENDEN. I move to lay the preamble and resolutions on the table.

Mr. MAY. On that motion I demand the yeas and nays.

The yeas and nays were ordered.

The question was taken; and it was decided in the affirmative—yeas 68, nays 44.

BILL TO RELEASE ALL STATE PRISONERS.

On the 13th of March, 1862, Mr. MAY reported from the Judiciary Committee, "A bill to provide for the discharge of State prisoners and others, and to authorize the judges of the United States Courts to take bail or recognizances to secure the trial of the same."

This bill was designed to restore the laws to all State and some military prisoners, and it provided the means of their speedy release without other conditions than giving bail such as the judge of their own judicial district might require. It passed the House, and is the bill that has given rise to so much debate in the Senate, but has been completely changed by amendments.

The only beneficial part of the "Indemnity Bill," as arranged by the Committee of Conference, and passed into a law—its second section, providing for the release of State prisoners who may not be indicted, is copied from the bill prepared by Mr. MAY, except the proviso requiring an oath of allegiance to the Government, &c.

FORT WARREN PROCEEDINGS.

Mr. MAY. I submit the following resolution, and move its adoption :

Resolved, That the Secretary of State be requested to communicate to this House a copy of an order which, on or about the 28th of November, 1861, he caused to be read to State prisoners confined in Fort Warren, whereby they were forbidden to employ counsel in their behalf, and informed that such employment of counsel would be regarded by the Government and by the State Department as a reason for prolonging the term of their imprisonment.

This was laid on the table, by yeas 63, nays 48.

CUSTOM-HOUSE IN BALTIMORE.

Mr. MAY submitted the following resolution :

WHEREAS, The Custom-House authorities of the city of Baltimore have imposed onerous and vexatious restrictions upon the internal trade and commerce of the people of Maryland among themselves, amounting in a great degree to a prohibition of the same, and discriminations are made in applying the said restrictions, by the discretion of the said authorities, of an unjust and mortifying character, and, in many instances, founded upon personal or political prejudices; and whereas, among others, it is required that citizens holding the faith of the Roman Catholic Church, as a condition of such trade and commerce, shall take and subscribe an oath discriminating against their religious faith, in the mode and ceremony of its administration, and this at a time when many thousands of soldiers holding the same faith are engaged in fighting the battles of the Government of the United States : and whereas, such discrimination is contrary to constitutional right, and is an odious reflection on the equality of religious privilege; and such restrictions are a violation of law, and a usurpation of the reserved rights of the people of Maryland exclusively to regulate and control their own internal trade and commerce, as the same has been decided by the Supreme Court of the United States, and such restrictions can only be justified, if at all, under military authority, and for reasons of military necessity—which do not exist—and the same are a manifest oppression of the people of Maryland; therefore,

Be it Resolved, 1. That the Secretary of the Treasury be requested to inform this House whether he has authorized or directed the said restrictions to be imposed; and, if so, to communicate a copy of his authority or order for the same, and all other information in his possession relating to the same.

2. That the Committee on the Judiciary be directed to inquire into the facts and legal authority of such proceedings, with power to send for persons and papers, and to report at an early day the result of its investigations.

This resolution was laid over.

The following, copied from the Baltimore *Republican* of the 17th March, is a proper sequel to the above resolution :

"A PORTION OF THE HISTORY OF THE TIMES."

"It will be remembered by many of our readers, that Mr. MAY, our Representative in the last Congress, submitted a resolution during the late session, in relation to the vexatious and unconstitutional restrictions imposed upon the trade of Baltimore, by the Custom House officers of this port. It will also be remembered, that Mr. MAY was attacked and denounced for having submitted the resolution referred to, and all that he stated was pronounced false and unfounded, and emanating solely from Mr. MAY's hostility to the old Know-Nothing party. One of the Government organs declared that they had visited the Custom House, and there ascertained positively, that no extra oaths were imposed upon Catholics or attempted to be imposed by any officer of the Customs. As a fair sample of the *truthfulness* of the journal referred to, we subjoin the report of the proceedings in the United States Court upon the very case referred to by Mr. MAY. These proceedings show that the Surveyor, Mr. McJILTON, did insist upon administering and oath to Mr. McALEER, *not authorized by the Constitution,* and because he refused to take such illegal oath, refused to pass his goods; hence the suit, the result of which we give below :"

UNITED STATES DISTRICT COURT.—Judge Giles.—United States *vs.* a lot of goods, wares and merchandise—Hugh McAleer, of Frederick, claimant. The grounds on which the goods were sought to be forfeited were, that a false statement had been made to obtain a permit. That the goods belonged to McAleer, and that they were passed through the Custom House to Mr. Obender, over the Baltimore and Ohio Railroad to Frederick, under a permit to Obender. The defense was based, first, on this being a case to which the laws of Congress and the regulations of the treasury, did not apply; second, is that if they did apply, McAleer was justified in obtaining them in the mode he did, because a discrimination had been made against him, growing out of his religion, as a Roman Catholic, which he could not yield to, without acquiescing in an insult to his religion, as well as an insult to him personally in this, that permits were refused to him as a Roman Catholic, unless he would make the oath usually required of those to whom permits were granted, with the addition of taking the same over the sign of the cross. The following witnesses were examined in the case :

*　　*　　*　　*　　*　　*　　*　　*

"Clinton Levering testified that the oath of McAleer, taken in Frederick, December 1st, (here exhibited the usual oath in the printed form,) was presented by him at the custom-house in this city, to the custom-house officer, Mr. McJilton, who told him he would not take McAleer's oath unless he would swear it over a cross, and gave witness a form which he had in a book at the custom-house, which form was longer than the usual form. Mr. McJilton said he would receive no oath from McAleer unless he would take it over a cross. Witness's impression was that Mr. McJilton thought Mr. McAleer would not regard an oath as binding unless over a cross, and that McJilton would require it of all Romanists. Do not think McJilton said anything about all Romanists; witness rather felt that there was something personal against McAleer; he so judged from what he had heard from clerks at the custom-house. Mr. McAleer on several occasions had presented a similar oath, and Mr. McJilton appeared annoyed that so many applications had been made to him. Mr. McJilton appeared excited. Mr. McAleer is a man of high character.

"Henry Whittington testified that he called at the custom-house with the oath, (here shown,) which was the one usually taken, as far as he knows. Mr. McJilton said no oath but one taken over a cross would do. In other words, he would not pass the goods in question unless the oath was taken over the sign of the cross. Witness has had goods passed under the oath he presented. He never heard any questions asked before.

*　　*　　*　　*　　*　　*　　*　　*

"The United States Attorney, after the above testimony, abandoned the case, and the jury then rendered a verdict in favor of the claimant, Mr. McAleer."

MILITARY INTERFERENCE WITH SLAVES.

Mr. MAY asked leave to offer the following resolutions:

WHEREAS, It is represented that certain military officers of the United States, stationed in Charles county, in the State of Maryland, have heretofore openly declared their purpose to set free from slavery, and remove them from said State, negro slaves owned therein under the laws thereof; and whereas, on the 5th day of January inst., the said military officers did assemble together, by the attractions of a band of music and other influences, a large number of said slaves in said county, and did openly entice and persuade them on board of a steamer belonging to, or in the service of the United States, and being at a place called Chapel Point, and did remove and transport said slaves by means of said steamer, from and beyond said State; and whereas, one Colonel Swain, commanding a regiment called "Scott's 900," acted a conspicuous part in the premises, and the same is a wanton and scandalous violation of the Constitution and laws of the United States and of the State of Maryland, and also of the duty of the said military officers, and a reckless aggression on the rights of the people of Maryland; therefore,

Be it Resolved, 1. That the President be requested to cause the above allegations to be investigated, and, if found true, to bring the offenders therein to punishment, and cause the said slaves to be restored to their owners, according to his duty.

2. That the Judiciary Committee be directed to inquire into the premises and report such legislation as may be necessary.

3. That a copy of this preamble and resolution be transmitted to the President.

Mr. LOVEJOY. I object.

The SPEAKER. The gentleman from Maryland having offered one resolution, cannot offer a second without consent, and the gentleman from Illinois objects.

The resolution was then ruled out.

EMANCIPATION IN MARYLAND.

Mr. BINGHAM, asked leave to introduce a bill granting aid to the State of Maryland for the purpose of securing the abolishment of slavery in said State.

Mr. MAY.—I object.

RESTRICTIONS ON THE INTERNAL TRADE OF MARYLAND.

Mr. MAY presented a memorial on this subject from James D. McCabe, H. M. Murray, Thomas J. Hall, and others, citizens of Anne Arundel county, Maryland, and referred it to the Judiciary Committee, of which Mr. MAY is a member. That committee referred the subject to Mr. MAY for investigation, who, after collecting all the facts, prepared an elaborate report in writing and read it to the Committee.

The principles announced in it received the approbation of Mr. PENDLETON, of Ohio, and Mr. THOMAS, of Massachusetts, members of that Committee. But a majority of the Committee refused to accept it as the report of the Committee, or to allow it to be made to the House as a minority report, or in any way to be presented to the House. The subject was strangled in the Committee.

It can hardly be necessary to add that this report fully exhibited the unconstitutional, unlawful, and oppressive character of the rules and regulations imposed upon the internal commerce of the people of Maryland by the Treasury Department and Custom-House authorities of Baltimore, and urged their immediate removal.

RIGHTS OF CONSCIENCE.

The following is a copy of Mr. MAY's resolution, referred to in his speech, and which, after repeated attempts made in vain, each day from the 16th of February, he at length succeeded in offering at the last moment of this Congress. Being read, they were objected to by the Republican side; Mr. MAY moved to suspend the rules in order to adopt them, and called the yeas and nays by the aid of the Democratic side, to make up the record on this vital question. As the Clerk commenced to call the yeas and nays, the hour of twelve on the 4th of March arrived, and the Speaker declared the House adjourned *sine die.*

It is an interesting and significant fact, that the popular branch of the 37th Congress terminated its existence, in a struggle—by the small but resolute minority—to maintain the rights of conscience against military tyranny.

Whereas, It is represented that Major General Schenck, commanding the forces of the United States stationed in Baltimore, Maryland, has ordered as a condition to be annexed to the worship of Almighty God, by certain religious societies or congregations of the Methodist Church of that city, that the flag of the United States "shall be conspicuously displayed" at the time and place of such worship.

And Whereas, The said order is a plain violation of "the inalienable right to worship God according to the dictates of every one's conscience," as it is asserted by the said congregations, and also by our declarations of fundamental rights, and as secured by our State and Federal Constitutions.

And Whereas, A minister of the said congregations, the Rev. John H. Dashiel, having, on Sunday, the 15th inst., removed the said flag from his own premises, which. was also the place of worship of one of said congregations, where the said flag had been placed surreptitiously by some evil-minded person, and for so doing was arrested by order of the said General Schenck, and held as a prisoner.

Be it Resolved, That the Judiciary Committee be, and hereby is instructed to inquire into the allegations aforesaid, and ascertain by what authority the said General Schenck exercises a power to regulate or interfere with the privileges of Divine worship, and also to arrest and detain as a prisoner the said minister of the Gospel, as aforesaid.

And, further, That said committee be instructed to report upon the same at an early day.

A conspicuous example of the futility and wickedness of an interference by government with the religious sentiments of a people, is furnished in the history of Herod, "who, fresh from the slaughter of the Innocents, made it the policy of his reign to undermine the faith of the people in the protection of God, as a defender distinct from the power of the Roman Empire; and as far as he could, he tried to overthrow and root out the spiritual work of Ezra. *He placed a gilt eagle, the Roman ensign, at the entrance to the temple;* and the Jews, irritated at this affront, rose in tumult and tore it down. This act of resistance cost three thousand of the people their lives."